CULTURES OF THE WORLD

Senegal

Elizabeth L. Berg and Ruth Wan

 Marshall Cavendish
Benchmark
New York

PICTURE CREDITS

© Nik Wheeler/Danita Delimont

AFP/AFP/Getty Images: 51 • Ariadne Van Zandbergen/Lonely Planet Images: 14 • Audrius Tomonis: 135 • Ben Radford/Getty Images: 111 • Bobby Haas/National Geographic Image Collection/Getty Images: 42 • Carik Bechwith/Angela Fisher/The Image Bank/Getty Images: 118 • Chip and Rosa Maria Peterson: 65, 76, 91, 92, 95 • Cynthia Johnson/Time Life Pictures/Getty Images: 36 • Dave G. Houser/Houserstock: 62 • David Else/Lonely Planet Images: 19, 48 • Diena/Brengola/Getty Images: 103 • Eric Feferberg/AFP/Getty Images: 30 • Eric Miller/i-Afrika:20, 22, 83, 113 • EyesWideOpen/Getty Images: 47 • Georges Gobet/AFP/Getty Images: 32, 120, 122 • Hutchison Library: 64, 115 • Isabelle Rozenbaum/Getty Images: 127 • Jason Laure: 60, 75, 102, 117 • Keystone/Hulton Archive/Getty Images: 105 • Matthew Schoenfelder/Lonely Planet Images: 94 • Nik Wheeler: 24, 100 • North Wind Picture Archives: 21 • photolibrary: 1, 5, 6, 11, 12, 18, 39, 41, 44, 55, 58, 67, 68, 71, 74, 79, 81, 82, 84, 98, 108, 114, 125, 126, 128, 129, 131 • Pierre Verdy/AFP/Getty Images: 31 • Pietro Scozzari: 2, 16, 17, 38, 50, 52, 59, 90, 101, 110 • Randy Olson/National Geographic Image Collection/Getty Images: 54 • Seyllou Diallo/AFP/Getty Images: 27, 29, 35, 37, 40, 57, 86, 93, 96, 107 • Topham Picturepoint: 9, 15, 26, 45, 70, 72, 99, 123, 124 • Trip Photographic Library: 10, 13, 33, 43, 46, 69, 85

PRECEDING PAGE

Portrait of a young Senegalese girl.

Publisher (U.S.): Michelle Bisson
Editors: Deborah Grahame, Stephanie Pee
Copyreader: Tara Koellhoffer
Designers: Nancy Sabato, Lynn Chin
Cover picture researcher: Connie Gardner
Picture researcher: Thomas Khoo

Marshall Cavendish Benchmark
99 White Plains Road
Tarrytown, NY 10591
Web site: www.marshallcavendish.us

© Times Media Private Limited 1997
© Marshall Cavendish International (Asia) Private Limited 2010
® "Cultures of the World" is a registered trademark of Times Publishing Limited.

Originated and designed by Marshall Cavendish International (Asia) Private Limited
An imprint of Marshall Cavendish International (Asia) Private Limited
A member of Times Publishing Limited

Marshall Cavendish is a trademark of Times Publishing Limited.

All Internet sites were correct and accurate at the time of printing. All monetary figures in this publication are in U.S. dollars.

Library of Congress Cataloging-in-Publication Data
Berg, Elizabeth, 1953-
  Senegal / by Elizabeth L. Berg and Ruth Lau. — 2nd ed.
    p. cm. — (Cultures of the world)
  Summary: "Provides comprehensive information on the geography, history, wildlife, governmental structure, economy, cultural diversity, peoples, religion, and culture of Senegal"—Provided by publisher.
  Includes bibliographical references and index.
  ISBN 978-0-7614-4481-7
  1. Senegal—Juvenile literature. I. Lau, Ruth. II. Title.
  DT549.22.B47 2010
  966.3—dc22   2009007067

Printed in China
7 6 5 4 3 2 1

CONTENTS

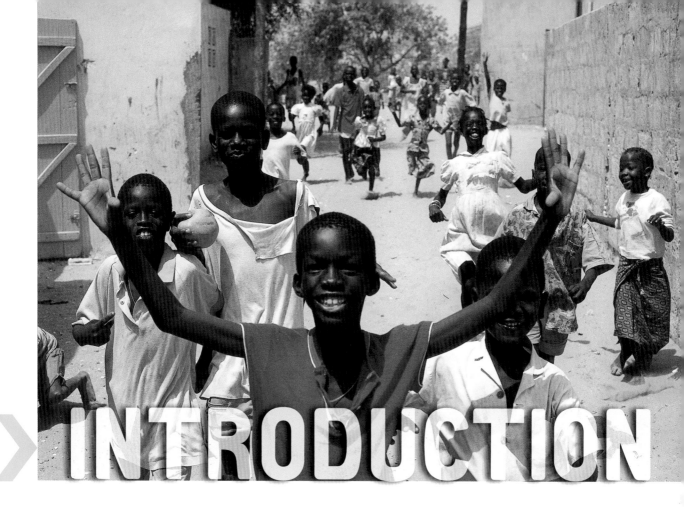

INTRODUCTION

SENEGAL IS NOT A typical African nation. **Since its independence** in 1960, it has seen peaceful transitions of power in a continent where coups, civil wars, and military rule are common. Senegal is often admired as one of the most stable democracies in Africa and a place where religious harmony—with the Muslim majority coexisting with the Christian and other religious minorities—and the arts, especially music and film, flourish. Although it is small, Senegal has much to be proud of, but in terms of the economy, Senegal continues to struggle. Senegal's dependence on foreign aid and imports for food and other basic necessities has continued. Poverty and unemployment, though less severe than they have been in the past, continue to be rife. Senegalese have shown themselves to be capable of resolving their own problems in even the toughest conditions. As a result Senegal continues to stand out as one of the lights of Africa.

GEOGRAPHY

Baobab trees.

S

ENEGAL IS AFRICA'S WESTERNMOST country. It is a flat, low-lying, arid land covering 75,955 square miles (196,722 square km). Roughly the size of the state of Nebraska, Senegal is bordered by Mauritania and Mali to the north and east, Guinea and Guinea-Bissau to the south, and on the west by the Atlantic Ocean. It almost entirely encircles the small country of The Gambia—an enclave that comprises the floodplain of the Gambia River.

Senegal lies in a depression known as the Senegal-Mauritanian Basin. Most of the land lies at altitudes under 330 feet (100 m), with a few areas of the Cape Verde peninsula and the southeast rising slightly higher. The coast is washed by the Canary Current, which keeps coastal temperatures mild, while the rest of the country experiences intense tropical heat.

Most of the population lives in the urban areas of the coastal region. The hinterland is composed of dry, flat plains with sparse vegetation. It is poor agricultural land, with rocky soil and little rain.

PHYSICAL FEATURES

Senegal is usually divided into five regions: the coastal region, the Senegal River Valley, the Ferlo, the eastern region, and the Casamance. The

The Casamance, which lies south of The Gambia, is markedly different from the rest of Senegal. Separated from the rest of the country by The Gambia, the Casamance has ample rainfall, making it a good area for growing rice and resulting in dense vegetation, including mangroves, thick forests, cashew nuts, and oil palms. This gradually changes to wooded or open savannah in the central and eastern parts of the Casamance.

The Casamance derives its name from the king (mansa, "MAHN-sah") of Kasa, who ruled the area when the Portuguese arrived. The oldest known inhabitants are the Diola—a group of small, dark-skinned people who probably migrated from the north. The Diola withdrew farther and farther into the forests in response to the arrival of new peoples, such as the Malinke, who also migrated to the region from the north. Few Diola live outside of Senegal. They are a fiercely independent people, many of whom still follow traditional animist beliefs, resisting both colonization and conversion. The Casamance was the last part of Senegal to be conquered by Europeans, and pockets of resistance were still active after World War I. This tradition of independence still continues, and the Casamance is the heart of a determined separatist struggle.

Diola traditions are very different from those of other Senegalese peoples. Traditionally egalitarian, Diola society is based on village self-rule, in contrast to some other Senegalese traditions—the Wolof, for instance, who emphasize a highly structured, hierarchical social organization. Diola are governed by two forces: public opinion and a belief in spirits that rule nature. Diola try to live in harmony with the surrounding environment and their fellow villagers, and to fulfill the social obligations that determine the well-being of the community.

coastal region stretches for 310 miles (500 km) along the Atlantic Ocean, extending as much as 15 miles (24 km) inland. The most prominent feature of the coast is the Cape Verde peninsula, the westernmost point in Africa. North of the Cape Verde peninsula, the coastal belt, called the Cayor, is characterized by small swamps or pools separated by sand dunes that may stand as high as 100 feet (30 m). South of Dakar, the coastal belt is narrower and consists of beaches flanked by low, wooded hills.

The repeated wash of the surf is slowly eroding the shores of Cape Verde.

The Senegal River Valley covers the northern part of Senegal. This region is a dry valley 10 miles (16 km) wide at the eastern end, expanding to 35 miles (56 km) as the river enters the coastal region. The vegetation is dependent on the annual flood cycle of the Senegal River. At the height of the flood, the water rises as high as the treetops, flooding villages. During the dry season, thirsty winds dry up all vegetation.

The broad plain in central Senegal is called the Ferlo. The area gets little rain, and the sandy soil does not hold moisture. Yellowed grass, scrub, and thorn trees are common to this area.

The eastern region is similar to the Ferlo, with poor seasonal pastures. This region is sparsely populated.

FLORA

Vegetation varies according to the region. The northern region is savannah woodland. Elephant grass is the most characteristic vegetation, although there are also fruit trees, such as mango, guava, orange, tangerine, grapefruit, coconut, papaya, and tamarind; hardwoods, such as mahogany and rosewood;

In this flat land, farmers in scattered villages eke out a living from small plots. Drought is common, and the neighboring Sahara slowly encroaches. Land that once supported numerous trees is beginning to lose all signs of vegetation.

Farmers tend to their small plot of land among the tall elephant grass.

as well as oil palms, rubber trees, and baobabs. These are used for charcoal and firewood, construction timber, and wood for sculpture.

The central region supports a variety of grassland and trees such as mahogany, shea, and kinkeliba (parts of which are used to reduce fevers). Vegetation that has adapted to a salty environment survives near the coasts. This includes salt cedars, acacia and mimosa trees, and clumps of salt grass. In the rest of the coastal region, vegetation is abundant, including oil palms, fruit trees, and garden vegetables.

The Casamance is heavily forested. Along the coast, mangrove thickets and groves of raffia and rattan palms fringe the estuaries. On higher ground, oil palms, mahogany, and teak can be found. Large areas have been cleared and converted to rice paddies.

FAUNA

Although Senegal is no longer home to the many wild animals that roam other parts of Africa, many large animals can still be found within the confines of

THE BAOBAB

The baobab tree is a distinctive feature of the West African landscape. Few villages are without an ancient baobab tree, some estimated to be more than 1,000 years old. The long, spindly branches gave rise to a Senegalese myth that the devil uprooted the baobab and plunged it back into the ground upside down.

The baobab can reach heights of 82.5 feet (25 m) and its huge, barrel-like trunk often reaches more than 30 feet (9 m) in girth, with a circumference of about 180 feet (54.5 m). Baobabs can also be found growing in some parts of India, although these do not grow nearly as tall as their African counterparts.

The baobab also has several unique properties that have added to its mystique. Unlike any other tree, it gets smaller rather than bigger as it grows older. It is able to store water in its trunk and, therefore, is highly valued by desert dwellers. The bark of the baobab is reported to cure malaria, while the leaves are eaten, or dried and powdered to make alo, *used to cure rheumatism and inflammation.*

The green mamba can be found in trees in Africa, and its venom is highly toxic.

Niokolo-Koba National Park. The park's 2,256,063 acres (913,000 hectares) provide a sanctuary for elephants, lions, leopards, hippopotami, warthogs, hyenas, jackals, gazelles and other antelope, and savannah monkeys. In other parts of the country, gazelles and antelope, wild pigs, small members of the cat family, monkeys, squirrels, hare, and rats can be found.

In addition, there are many poisonous snakes in the Casamance, including pythons, vipers, cobras, and mambas. The green mamba is exceptionally dangerous.

There are crocodiles and fish in the Senegal River and the Upper Gambia. One of the most important fish found in the Senegal River is the Nile perch. Saltwater food species, such as prawns and oysters, can be found far upstream due to the seasonal ebb and flow of the water.

Birds include local species and migrants from colder climates. The estuaries of the rivers are home to cormorants, herons, egrets, ducks, terns, and pelicans. Queleas forage for grain in nearby grain fields. In drier areas, there are secretary birds, bustards, and ostriches.

Insects are a major problem in Senegal. Mosquitoes, which carry malaria, yellow fever, and dengue, are common in most areas. The tsetse fly carries a parasite that causes sleeping sickness in horses, cattle, and humans. It is found in the humid, wooded areas in southern Senegal. Grasshoppers, plant lice, and termites are major crop pests throughout the country.

CLIMATE

Senegal has a tropical climate characterized by high daytime temperatures and a long dry season. Near the coast, temperatures are moderate, rarely falling below 60°F (16°C). The Canary Current off the coast keeps temperatures in the coastal zone milder than in the rest of the country. Inland temperatures may reach as high as 100°F (38°C) during the day. There is little seasonal variation, since the country is close to the equator.

The wide variety of wildlife housed in the confines of Niokolo-Koba National Park makes it a major tourist attraction in Senegal. Buffaloes, gazelles, black antelope, bushbucks, roan antelope, waterbucks, cobs, duikers, hippopotami, lions, apes, crocodiles, and warthogs are just a few of the species that are commonly seen.

The dry wind that blows from the Sahara desert during the dry season is called the harmattan.

The Gambia River flows through Senegal before reaching The Gambia.

The year is divided into rainy and dry seasons. The wet season lasts from May to November. Annual rainfall ranges from 10 inches (25 cm) in the north to 25 inches (63 cm) in Dakar and 60 inches (150 cm) in the Casamance. The dry season, by contrast, is practically rainless.

West Africa experiences *tornades* ("tohr-NAHD"), storms that bring thunder, lightning, and wind squalls. These do not last long but are followed by torrential rain that lasts one to two hours.

RIVERS

Senegal's rivers are sluggish and swampy. The Senegal River originates in the Fouta Djallon mountains in Guinea, flowing northeast 990 miles (1,600 km) to Mali, then turning west into Senegal, where it forms the northern border with Mauritania. The Senegal River divides the Sahara from the lands to the south. It is navigable for 175 miles (110 km) from the Atlantic Ocean to Podor, Senegal, all year-round. The river is navigable all the way to Kayes in Mali during the rainy season. During the dry season, ocean tides flow almost 300 miles (485 km) upstream, due to low water levels. Dams have helped control the ebb and flow of the tides. The most important is the dam and gate on the Taoue channel, which created the Lac de Guiers.

The Gambia River also rises in Guinea, flowing through the Senegal for 700 miles (1,100 km) before reaching The Gambia. The Casamance River is slow moving for most of its 200 miles (320 km).

CITIES

About 42 percent of Senegal's population resides in urban areas, which are concentrated in the coastal region, leaving a vast underpopulated hinterland. Besides Dakar and Saint-Louis, major cities include Kaolack in the peanut growing area, Thiès, Rufisque, and Ziguinchor, the main city of the Casamance.

Boulevard Général de Gaulle is one of the main avenues in Dakar.

DAKAR is the capital of Senegal and one of the leading cities of West Africa. Located at the westernmost point of Africa, Dakar is ideally situated as a major trading center.

Once the administrative hub of French West Africa, today Dakar is one of the most important seaports of Africa, large enough to accommodate 40 to 50 oceangoing vessels at one time. The port is also equipped with repair services, refrigerated warehouses, and pipelines for oil and liquid chemicals.

Dakar's population was 20,000 in 1900. It grew to 300,000 in 1960, and today the city of Dakar has about 1 million people and the metropolitan area of Dakar has 2.5 million people. Construction of government housing developments has not kept pace with urban migration, and overcrowding is a major problem.

An aerial view of the capital city of Dakar.

Clothes dry along a street in Saint-Louis.

Dakar is a blend of old and new styles of architecture. Modern office and apartment buildings have grown up alongside the colonial buildings and wide avenues constructed by the French.

SAINT-LOUIS Senegal's third-largest city and second-largest seaport was an early French settlement in Senegal, founded by colonists in 1659. For most of the colonial period it served as the capital of French West Africa. It was one of the centers of the slave trade.

After the construction of the Dakar-Saint-Louis railway in 1885, Dakar eclipsed Saint-Louis as the trading and administrative center of Senegal. The age of French colonial glory, however, has left the city with a legacy of colonial architecture that is unmatched in Africa, dating from the 1700s. Today Saint-Louis is the regional capital of north Senegal.

HISTORY

An old colonial house on the street of Saint-Louis is a reminder of Senegal's past.

BEFORE THE SAHARA began expanding to the south and west, West Africa was covered with lush vegetation and a profusion of game. Sometime before 800 B.C., nomadic tribes began to migrate to the area. Gradually hunting, fishing, and crop cultivation replaced the nomadic lifestyle.

Groups of megaliths near the mouth of the Senegal River attest to the religious life of early peoples. These stones vary in height from 3 feet (1 m) to 12 feet (3.5 m). One group contains 54 stone circles, each circle measuring 18 feet (5.5 m) in diameter. Just outside most of the circles, on the east side, is a Y-shaped stone. To an observer standing in the center of the circle, the sun would appear to rise over this stone at the winter solstice, thus marking the beginning of the sun's return. Skeletons have been found buried in these circles, giving rise to the theory that these megaliths were used as burial grounds for royalty and priests.

EARLY KINGDOMS

Near the end of the third century, the first major West African civilization, the Ghana Empire, made its appearance. The Ghana Empire gradually spread west from its center in Mali to include parts of what is today Senegal. Located at an

Right: Megaliths found in the Senegambian region give historians an idea of the religious lives of early peoples.

19

Muslims from North Africa came to the Senegalese region to buy slaves.

important crossroads of African trade, the Ghana Empire became rich from trade in gold, slaves, and ivory. It dominated the Senegambia region until the 10th century.

In the ninth century, the Tukulor people established the powerful Tekrur Empire. In the 11th century the empire converted to Islam. In 1076 Muslim Almoravids from North Africa joined with Tekrur to defeat the Ghana Empire, and Islam became the dominant force in the region.

One of the most important kingdoms in this area was the Mali Empire, which reached its peak in the early 14th century under the reign of Mansa Moussa. Centered in the eastern part of Senegal, the Mali Empire extended over most of Western Africa. By the late 14th century, however, the Mali Empire was in decline. Soon a new power would assert itself in the region.

THE JOLOF EMPIRE

The Wolof date their beginnings to the legendary King Njajan Njai of Jolof in the 13th century. According to legend, Njajan Njai emerged from a lake to settle a dispute between two tribes and then disappeared again. The people wanted him to be their king, so they started another fight. When he reappeared, they sent their most beautiful women to entice him to stay. Thus he became king of the Wolof. He led the Wolof in battle against the neighboring states of Waalo, Cayor, Bawol, Sine, and Saloum, conquering and incorporating them into the Jolof Empire.

The Jolof Empire reached its height in the 15th century, extending from the mouth of the Senegal River to modern Thiès and stretching 150 miles (240 km) into the interior. The kingdom's economy was based on cattle, millet, slaves, horses, and cloth.

THE EUROPEANS ARRIVE

In 1444 Portuguese navigators reached Cape Verde. Establishing a trading center at the mouth of the Senegal River, the Portuguese began a profitable trade in slaves and gold. Gradually the Dutch, French, and English also set up shop. Manufactured goods such as glassware, jewelry, cutlery, textiles, and weapons, as well as luxury items such as tobacco and liquor, were

Slaves were manacled and carried via slave ships to the New World.

traded to the African rulers in exchange for malagueta pepper, hides, gum arabic (used for making paper, candy, and textiles), gold, and slaves.

The Europeans were welcomed as trading partners but not as residents. They were only permitted to settle in specified areas, and their travel was restricted. As an exception, some Portuguese were allowed to settle and marry local women.

In the seventh century the French established their first permanent settlement in Senegal, on Gorée Island. Explorers such as Mungo Park began to explore the interior of the country. When the French lost their colonies in the New World and Asia, their interest in Western Africa grew. In 1840 the French government declared Senegal a permanent French possession and established an administration there.

Cannons dating back to the 17th century can still be found on Gorée Island.

FRENCH WEST AFRICA

In 1848 the French government granted all Senegalese born in the communes of Dakar, Gorée, Rufisque, and Saint-Louis French citizenship. French policy in the colony was governed by the principle of "assimilation." In this view, Africans were inferior people without any valuable civilization. The object of French policy, therefore, was to impart French culture to them, gradually assimilating them into French society. The administration opened schools complete with French curriculum, offered scholarships for Africans to study in France, and attempted to convert the Senegalese to French ways. These attempts to assimilate the Senegalese were largely successful

GORÉE ISLAND AND THE SLAVE TRADE

Africans had held and traded slaves throughout most of their history. Captives obtained in wars became the household slaves of rulers or were sold to Muslim traders. Generally these slaves were well treated, much the same as any worker. Slaves were adopted into the household. An intelligent and enterprising slave might marry into the owner's family and inherit his property, or become a trusted advisor or military leader. The children of slaves were considered free. Initially the Portuguese continued in this same vein, sending slaves back to Portugal as household servants or to sugar plantations on the islands off the coast of West Africa.

However, in the 16th century, slavery took a different turn. The large plantations in the New World required massive numbers of laborers. The New World peoples proved unable to withstand the grueling conditions, and so African slaves became the cornerstone of this new economy. Between 1500 and 1850 more than 12 million Africans were taken as slaves to the New World. These Africans endured conditions among the worst that have ever been inflicted upon human beings. Large numbers of them were from Senegambia, although the region ranked behind Dahomey, the Niger Delta, and Angola in total numbers of slaves exported. This went on until 1848, when a new republican government in France abolished slavery.

The main departure point for the slave ships was Gorée Island off the coast of Dakar. Gorée Island changed hands repeatedly during the colonial period, from Portugal to Holland, to France, to England, and back to France, but no matter who was the master, for 200 years it remained a center of the slave trade. Here Africans were held in slave warehouses before being shipped across the Atlantic on the dehumanizing Middle Passage. The Middle Passage was the brutal and horrific transportation of Africans across the Atlantic to the plantations of the Caribbean and Americas. Africans were captured and imprisoned in forts, or barracoons, on the coast before enduring the inhumane conditions of the Middle Passage, or the "way of death." Tens of thousands of men, women, and children stayed in the slave houses of Gorée. Many never left the ship alive, and those who did faced a challenging fate on the other side of the ocean.

In 1951 Gorée Island was declared a historical site and its buildings were preserved for their historical value. Today it is an important site for African-American tourists visiting Africa, but also for politicians from many countries.

Old-style French colonial houses still line the streets in many Senegalese towns.

among the upper classes during the early stages of French colonization. Children of rich parents were given the opportunity to study in Paris, opening a whole new world to them. Among the lower classes resistance was much stronger. The French administration soon encountered strong resistance from Muslim leaders, who saw in the French presence a threat to their authority. Muslim leaders such as Lat Dyor and Al-Hajj Umar Tal continued to wage jihads, Islamic holy wars, against the French well into the 1880s. The Diola in the Casamance continued their resistance to colonial rule into the 20th century.

In 1852 a man arrived in Senegal who would single-handedly shape the colony of French West Africa. Two years after his arrival, Major Louis Faidherbe became governor of the colony. During his term as governor, he put down resistance to French rule, extended French territory in the region, founded Dakar, established a French language newspaper, founded the Bank of Senegal, raised funds for the building of a railroad linking Dakar with Saint-Louis, and promoted the raising of peanuts as a cash crop.

In 1889 Britain negotiated control of the Gambia River Valley, while the French took over the Casamance region from Portugal. By 1900 the Federation of French West Africa extended east to Niger, into Dahomey, Chad, the Ivory Coast, Guinea, Upper Volta, and north into Mauritania, Algeria, and Tunisia. Covering 3.29 million square miles (8.5 million square

RESISTANCE

Resistance to French domination was widespread in the Senegambian region. It was led primarily by marabouts, or religious leaders, who had replaced traditional leaders as local headmen. The most important of these was Al-Hajj Umar Tal, a Tukulor marabout. He returned from a pilgrimage to Mecca in 1833, fired with zeal to convert the pagans to Islam. After many years of preparation, he launched a jihad, or holy war, during which he forcibly converted a vast tract of Senegal and Mali before Louis Faidherbe, the colonial governor, finally crushed him. He is today remembered as an important freedom fighter, despite the fact that much of his energy was directed against other Senegalese people.

Lat Dyor was another source of inspiration to Senegalese resistance. He became king of Cayor, the most important kingdom in the Senegal region, in 1862. Born animist, Lat Dyor converted to Islam. Concerned about the construction of a railroad, Lat Dyor dedicated himself to ridding the area of French colonialists. He continued a holy war against them until his death in 1886.

km), it was the largest colonial region in Africa. Saint-Louis was the administrative hub of the colony.

INDEPENDENCE

In 1914 Blaise Diagne became Senegal's first black African deputy in the French parliament, a post he would hold until his death in 1934. In 1946 Léopold Sédar Senghor succeeded Diagne in the National Assembly. Senghor was Senegal's only Catholic president, of a predominantly Muslim country. These two events were great milestones on the road to independence for Senegal.

During World War II, the Senegalese soldiers fought at the side of their French counterparts. After the war was over, France announced the formation of a French Union. French colonies overseas were offered membership in the newly created union, which would bring greater representation for the colonies in the French parliament.

In 1984 Léopold Senghor was elected a member of the French Academy, an honorary society of writers and intellectuals. He was the first African to receive that honor.

LÉOPOLD SENGHOR

Léopold Sédar Senghor (1906—2001) is a product of mixed Serer, Fulani, and Malinke heritage. The son of a Serer trader, he attended a Catholic mission in the hopes of becoming a priest, but later decided that the priesthood was not for him. In 1928 he went to Paris on a scholarship to continue his studies. There he was struck by the importance of African influence on modern painting, a fact that led him to reconsider the significance of African history and culture.

In the face of prevailing French precepts of African inferiority, Senghor became a major architect of the doctrine of "Negritude," which proclaimed the value of African culture and experience. As president he adopted the doctrine of Negritude as the basis for the government of Senegal, gradually revamping the institutions of the new country to better reflect the needs of its African population, and replacing French personnel with Africans. His personal prestige helped establish Senegal's reputation as a progressive, stable, and democratic country during the early years of independence.

Senghor developed stability and cooperation through strong ties with community leaders, offering favors in return for the votes of their communities. Although he sneered at what he called la politique politicienne *("politicians' politics"), he was a skilled and clever politician himself, and manipulated his opponents in order to achieve his aims.*

Senghor was a distinguished poet and is considered one of the foremost figures of Francophone literature. In his poetry he expresses his feelings about France, Africa, and colonization. His collections include Chants d'Ombre (Shadow Songs, *1945),* Hosties Noires (Black Offerings, *1948),* Ethiopiques *(1956),* Nocturnes *(1961),* Lettres d'Hivernage (Winter Letters, *1973),* La Poesie de L'action: Conversation Avec Mohamed Aziza *(1980), and* Ce Que Je Crois *(1988). He helped found* Présence Africaine *(African Presence), the principal journal of African Francophone culture.*

In April 1960 Senegal became part of the Mali Federation, which included Senegal and the area that is now Mali. The Mali Federation only lasted four and a half months before a struggle for power resulted in Senegal's secession from the union on August 20, 1960. After helping his country along the route to independence, Léopold Senghor served as Senegal's first president, leading the newly created republic from 1960 until his retirement in 1980.

POST-INDEPENDENCE

Following the breakup of the Mali Federation, President Senghor and Prime Minister Mamadou Dia governed together under a parliamentary system. Almost immediately this dual structure proved to be a problem. A power struggle between Senghor and Dia ended with the elimination of the office of prime minister and Dia's imprisonment, after the army stepped in to support Senghor. From 1964 to 1975 Senghor ruled the country without opposition, establishing an international image of peace and stability.

Former Prime Minister, Mamadou Dia.

In 1970 Senghor reestablished the office of prime minister and appointed Abdou Diouf, a young Socialist Party technocrat. Declaring his desire for a gradual return to multiparty politics, Senghor amended the constitution in 1976, allowing three parties, representing democratic socialist, liberal democratic, and Marxist-Leninist persuasions. In January 1981 Senghor stepped down, and Diouf became the president.

THE CASAMANCE PROBLEM

Since 1982 the Diola people of the Casamance have been in a state of armed rebellion led by the Mouvement des Forces Démocratiques de Casamance, *or MFDC—Movement of Democratic Forces in the Casamance. The rebellion was sparked by a revolt of* lycée (high school) *students in 1981, followed by a larger demonstration in front of the governor's mansion in Ziguinchor, during which the Senegalese flag was replaced by the flag of the Casamance movement. Since then there have been regular riots and armed attacks almost every year. Attempts to reach a settlement have so far produced no lasting results, although ceasefires have been declared many times. For example, a ceasefire agreement in 1997 did not prevent the death toll from increasing between 1997 and 2000, with a total of about 500 killed during those years. In March 2001 MFDC's leader, Father Diamacoune Senghor, signed a new peace deal that fell short of full autonomy for Casamance. This deepened the rift between MFDC hardliners and moderates and the occasional uprisings and street ambushes have continued until today, despite the latest peace deal signed in 2004. In addition, land mines laid by separatist rebels have rendered about 80 percent of Casamance unusable.*

The MFDC takes its name from a former regional political party that joined Léopold Senghor's party before independence. In addition to a long history of resistance to outside interference in the Casamance, there are many other points of contention with the Wolof-dominated Senegal government. The Casamance, largely neglected by the national government, particularly in areas of infrastructure development, has been invaded by merchants and bureaucrats from the north who have tried to impose their language and religion on the Diola.

Diouf immediately amended the constitution to admit all opposition parties and abolished the post of prime minister. Marking a distinct departure from the Senghor era, Diouf declared Senegal an Islamic nation and took an active role in pan-African politics.

However, he soon encountered major problems at home. In 1981 the Mouvement des Forces Démocratiques de Casamance (MFDC) initiated

Former President Abdoulaye Wade (left) shakes hands with founder of the Movement of Democratic Forces in the Casamance, Father Diamacoune Senghor, when they met in 2004 to sign a peace pact.

an armed independence struggle in the Casamance. The conflict, which has resulted in significant loss of life, remains unresolved despite several attempted ceasefires.

In 1982 Senegal joined with The Gambia to form a confederation called Senegambia. Common policies were established in areas of defense and security, external relations, communication, and information. Most important was the attempt at economic cooperation. However, this union was dissolved in 1989 when relations between the two countries deteriorated.

SENEGAL TODAY

Former President of Senegal Abdou Diouf served four terms before President Abdoulaye Wade was elected.

Abdou Diouf served four terms as president before being replaced by Abdoulaye Wade in 2000 through democratic elections. Wade was 74 years old at that time, and his victory meant the end of the rule of the Socialist Party, of which the two previous presidents, Diouf and Senghor, had been members. In 2001 Wade's Senegalese Democratic Party gained control of the National Assembly, winning 89 out of 120 seats. This further strengthened Wade's position as president. That same year, a new constitution was approved with 90 percent of the electoral vote. Among other things, it reintroduced and enhanced the role of the prime minister and reduced the president's term from seven to five years.

In 2002 Senegal experienced a national tragedy when the MS *Joola*, a ferry connecting Dakar and Ziguinchor, the Casamance capital, capsized, leaving 1,863 people dead. The sinking of the MS *Joola* is the African continent's largest maritime disaster to date. Wade said that the country would assume responsibility for the sinking and dismissed his prime minister, Idrissa Seck, and cabinet in response. It was later revealed that the MS *Joola* had been carrying three times the number of passengers it was licensed to.

Wade won reelection in February 2007, garnering 56 percent of the vote. He has a strong interest in raising Senegal's regional and international profile, helping to launch the New Partnership for Africa's Development (NEPAD), a plan that aims to foster economic recovery through African-led reform and good governance in 2001. Wade has also been pushing for privatization and market-opening measures in the economy.

A NOTORIOUS GUEST

Senegal has been home to Hissene Habre since 1992. Habre was the leader of Chad for nine years and fled to Senegal with millions of dollars after being ousted. He has been accused of numerous human rights abuses, including political killings, torture, and disappearances. A Senegalese court indicted Habre in 2000, but subsequently, the court said it had no authority to prosecute him on charges of torture. In April 2008 Senegal's national assembly amended the country's constitution to allow the trial of Habre.

However, critics say he has not fully delivered on his election promises to raise the standard of living in Senegal. Although Wade has improved the infrastructure of Senegal, building a new highway along the coast and setting out plans to transform Dakar into a high-tech regional hub, international agencies, such as the International Monetary Fund (IMF) and World Bank, have criticized him for not doing enough to address the basic concerns of people on the ground, such as rising food prices. Unemployment also continues to be rife and a large majority of Senegalese continue to live in slums where they experience regular blackouts and unclean water and sanitation.

In a 2008 Gallup survey, 56 percent of Senegalese polled said they would leave Senegal permanently if they could. In recent years one major challenge has been to stem the mass migration of Senegalese, usually young men, who set sail for Europe for a better life. Senegal has become a favorite starting point for such illegal immigrants who usually head to the Canary Islands in search of jobs. The journey is perilous, as rickety wooden boats are often used, and it is estimated that one in six illegal immigrants die during the trip.

President Abdoulaye Wade attends the World Economic Forum in January 2009.

GOVERNMENT

Children hold up posters of Senegalese Prime Minister Macky Sall during a campaign meeting in 2007.

CHAPTER 3

SENEGAL IS A SECULAR REPUBLIC with a resilient history of democratic multiparty politics and civilian rule. Although the first 20 years of its history as an independent nation were dominated by one man, Léopold Senghor, power was handed over smoothly to Abdou Diouf in 1980 when Senghor stepped down before his fifth term as president ended.

Likewise Diouf graciously stepped down after losing the presidential election to Abdoulaye Wade in 2000, ending 40 years of domination by the Socialist Party. In a continent plagued by political turmoil and election fraud, Senegal's peaceful transitions of power are no small feats. In fact Senegal is the only West African nation and one of the few African nations not to have experienced a coup d'etat since independence.

THE PRESIDENT

The president of Senegal is the head of state and the prime minister is the head of government. The president is elected by direct and universal suffrage, the voting age being 18 years old. Based on

Right: Guards outside the presidential palace in Dakar.

Senegal is a semi-presidential, liberal democratic republic. The people vote to elect the president. Senegal's government has been spared much of the political conflict that plagues many of its neighbors.

on the new constitution of 2001, the president's term of office is five years and he can serve for a maximum of two terms. The president appoints the prime minister and together they appoint the cabinet, some members of the Senate, and the justices.

THE PARLIAMENT AND LOCAL ADMINISTRATION

Senegal's parliament is bicameral, meaning it has two parts: the National Assembly and the Senate. The National Assembly consists of 150 members who are elected by direct and universal suffrage, whereas the Senate's 100 members are in part appointed by the president and in part elected by local councillors and deputies. The presidential election and the election of the National Assembly, also known as parliamentary or legislative elections, are held separately.

Senegal is divided into 11 administrative regions, which are then divided into 34 *départements* ("DAY-pahr-tay-mahn") and 103 *arrondissements* ("AH-rohn-deese-mahn"). The regions are administered by governors, who are assisted by deputy governors, one in charge of administration and the other of development. A regional assembly handles local taxation, and each region maintains a separate budget. Dakar is governed by an elected municipal council.

POLITICAL PARTIES

The constitution provides for a multiparty system, although from 1960 to 2000 the Socialist Party dominated Senegal's political scene, with the first

Supporters of the Socialist Party in Dakar.

two presidents, Léopold Senghor and Abdou Diouf, being members of that party. Today about 72 parties representing socialist, liberal, and Marxist positions are active.

THE ROLE OF THE MILITARY

Senegal's active armed forces total 17,000 men, in addition to a 4,000-strong military gendarmerie. A *gendarmerie* is a police station in France and French-speaking countries. Military service lasts two years and is by selective conscription. Conscription is a compulsory enrollment of personnel for service in the armed forces. The military receives training and equipment from the United States, France, and, to a smaller extent, Germany.

Unlike many African countries, the Senegalese military has generally refrained from becoming involved in politics, although military intervention

Senegalese troops await inspection.

in the power struggle between Senghor and Mamadou Dia in 1963 (in which army support for Senghor determined the outcome of the conflict) indicates the potential for involvement. In other circumstances, the army has ignored the opposition's requests for intervention.

However, the Senegalese military has aided and intervened in the conflicts of its neighbors. In 1981 the Senegalese military accepted an invitation from then-Gambian President Dawda Kairaba Jawara to step in and quell a coup attempt in Gambia. In 1998 the Senegalese military once again intervened, this time in Guinea-Bissou, to aid in a civil war at the request of then-President Joao Bernardo Vieiva.

The Senegalese military has actively participated in international and regional peacekeeping and peace-support missions. In 1991 Senegal was the only sub-Saharan nation to send a contingent to participate in Operation Desert Storm in the Middle East. Today Senegal has deployed 2,000 troops on United Nations (UN) peacekeeping and peace-support missions, including 840 soldiers in Darfur and others in Liberia and the Democratic Republic of Congo.

FOREIGN RELATIONS

Senegal's ties with France have remained strong since independence. In fact, France is one of the greatest contributors of economic aid to Senegal. Under President Wade, Senegal also enjoys strong relations with the United States, where a sizable population of overseas Senegalese reside. Like France, the United States provides considerable economic and technical assistance to Senegal.

In terms of its neighbors, Senegal has experienced strained relations with Mauritania since a border dispute over animal grazing rights erupted in the Senegal River Valley and spawned a two-year border conflict (1989—91) replete with looting, bloodshed, and more than 250,000 persons forced into exile. Although the dispute was settled in 1991, Senegal continues to house 30,000 refugees who only recently began to return to Mauritania, in late 2007. Senegal is also a large market for French products and Francophone literature and media. The French military retains bases in Senegal.

Senegalese interior minister Ousmane Ngom (right) and French minister for immigration and co-development Brice Hortefeux (left) examine a sword. Ties between Senegal and France continue to be strong.

ECONOMY

Women at work in the padi fields.

CHAPTER 4

>S ENEGAL'S ECONOMY HAS faced many challenges since its independence. A prolonged drought in the early 1970s led to severe food shortages that resulted in the government incurring a large foreign debt. The unemployment rate was at 20 percent in the late 1980s, and in 1994 the Senegalese government was forced to admit that it was on the verge of bankruptcy.

Under pressure from international donors, particularly the International Monetary Fund (IMF) and the World Bank, then-President Diouf was forced to devalue the Senegalese currency, the CFA franc, by 50 percent—a drastic measure strongly resisted in Senegal. However, in the

A beggar counts coins. Poverty is rampant in Senegal, and many people resort to begging to support themselves.

In comparison to other African nations, Senegal's economy is perceived to be healthy. However, about half of its working population remains unemployed and it still depends heavily on foreign aid. Fishing and agriculture make up two of Senegal's main economic activities, but overfishing, poor soil quality, and harsh environmental conditions threaten them.

Demonstrators take to the streets to protest the rising cost of living in Senegal.

aftermath of the devaluation, the government was successful in controlling inflation and the budget deficit, and in meeting debt repayment obligations.

Today Senegal's economic report card is a mixed bag. Senegal is considered a good economic performer by the World Bank, with the fourth-largest economy in West Africa, after Nigeria, Ghana, and Côte d'Ivoire. Admirably it has achieved an annual growth rate of about 5 percent since its currency devaluation in 1994, and poverty has declined from 68 percent in 1994 to 51 percent in 2005. However, Senegal remains a poor country with unemployment hovering around 48 percent for the past few years. The average worker earns only $840 a month and Senegal continues to rely heavily on foreign assistance, which comprises 23 percent of annual government spending, or $630 million, from countries and organizations such as France, United States, European Union, China, the IMF, World Bank, and the African Development Bank.

FISHING

Senegal's fishing sector contributes the largest amount of export earnings to the economy—about $366 million in 2005. Senegal exports fish such as tuna, shrimp, sardines, salmon, anchovies, and hake, mainly to countries in the European Union where such fish are popular foods. Both the export of fish and the sale of fishing rights to foreign countries, in particular European Union countries such as Spain, Portugal, and Greece, have made the fishing sector an increasingly valuable source of income for Senegal. The fishing sector employs about 600,000 people, or about 17 percent of Senegal's workforce. Fish is also a main part of the Senegalese diet. The Senegalese consume twice as much fish as people in other parts of the world.

Fishing is an important source of revenue for the Senegalese.

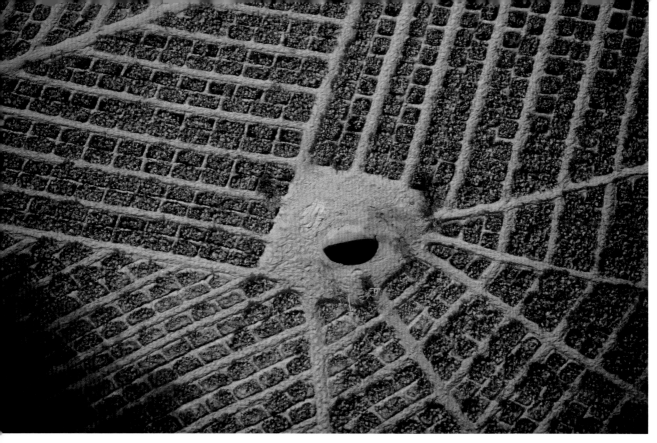

An aerial view of crops around a well.

In recent times overfishing has been resulting in the depletion of fish stock in Senegal's offshore waters, which is a serious concern. In addition, fish exported from Senegal faces competition from fish from Asian countries, where the fishing industries may be more efficient and cost-effective. Chinese fishing boats also contribute to the problem of depleting West Africa's fish supplies.

AGRICULTURE

Agriculture contributes 16 percent of Senegal's gross domestic product (GDP) and supports about 77.5 percent of Senegal's workforce. Agricultural production in Senegal is largely focused on cash crops, the main ones being groundnuts, cotton, gum arabic, and sugarcane. Groundnuts have been Senegal's dominant agricultural product for a long time. They take up 40 percent of the cultivated land in Senegal, or about 2.4 million acres

(1 million ha). About 661,387 tons (600,000 tonnes) of groundnuts are produced annually, and the groundnut farming industry employs about one million people. However, the fishing sector has replaced the groundnut sector as Senegal's export leader since 2005—the export of groundnuts only earns Senegal $63 million annually, and this figure is declining.

Agriculture has been limited by inadequate farming methods, a low level of soil fertility, periodic droughts, and plagues of locusts. Outside the Senegal River floodplain, soils are not very rich. In fact, only 12.5 percent of Senegal's land is arable. In addition, there is little rainfall, most of which falls between June and September. Today agricultural productivity is not sufficient to feed the people living on the land, much less provide a surplus to feed the cities. In 2005 Senegal imported 936,965 tons (850,000 tonnes) of rice, 330,693 tons (300,000 tonnes) of wheat, and 220,462 tons (200,000 tonnes) of fruits and vegetables. Senegal is the second-largest importer of grains in Africa and one of the world's top food importers. In an effort to address the insufficiency of agricultural productivity, the government launched the Great Agricultural Offensive for Food and Abundance in 2008. This is a national strategy to make Senegal self-sufficient in food by 2015. Its key strategies are to offer tax breaks to foreign countries to grow food in Senegal, improve the irrigation and cultivation of unused land near the Senegal River, and ramp up the production of rice, a staple of the Senegalese people.

Women play an active part in the cultivation of crops in Senegal.

Cattle are a valuable commodity for bartering during hard times.

LIVESTOCK

The livestock sector contributes 5.5 percent of the GDP. Local farmers and households raise 3,000 cattle, 8,400 sheep and goats, 45,000 poultry, and 300 pigs. Cattle are raised in most areas of Senegal, but they do not constitute a major source of income for farmers. Livestock are considered symbols of dignity and personal status, especially among the Fulani, who are traditionally herders. The average Senegalese family relies more on goats and sheep than cattle for food and income. Horses are raised as draft animals and for transportation. A scarcity of safe water supplies poses a problem for both humans and livestock.

INDUSTRY AND RESOURCES

Compared to other West African countries, Senegal has a fairly well-developed industrial sector. Principal industries are groundnut-oil processing, cement and shoe plants, textile mills, chemicals, paper, furniture, and electrical products. Imports include food and beverages, consumer goods, capital goods, and petroleum. The main exports are fish, phosphates, groundnuts, petroleum products, and cotton. Senegal also has a plastic industry with at least two Lebanese-run factories and a large market domestically and in neighboring West African countries.

Senegal's mineral resources consist of phosphates of lime in the area northeast of Dakar and aluminum phosphates near Thiès. The government has successfully encouraged the development of the phosphate industry, and phosphate production contributes $230 million annually in export earnings to the economy, second only to the export of fish, which contributes $249 million.

Resources yet to be exploited include petroleum deposits off the coast of the Casamance and high-grade iron ore in the upper Faleme Valley. There are saltworks at Kaolack. Gum arabic (from acacia trees) and other forest products are less important. The coast has titanium-filled sand that yields zircon, a mineral used in gem-making.

Workers fill sacks of millet at a factory in Saint-Louis.

TOURISM

Senegal strongly promotes tourism as a critical growth industry. Dakar and the beautiful islands of Ile de Goree and Iles de la Madeleine in the Cape Verde Peninsula welcome visitors with exciting night life and stunning beaches. Coastal and rural villages south of Dakar, in the regions of Thiès and Ziguinchor, also draw large numbers of tourists each year. Likewise northern Senegal with its big historic city of Saint-Louis and national parks such as Parc National des Oiseaux du Djoudj and Parc National de la Langue de Barbarie are popular tourist destinations. All in all, Senegal has 250 tourist-class hotels and employs 100,000 people in the tourism sector.

Tourists visit a *campement* bird park at Djoudj.

Senegalese pack onto a crowded bus in Dakar.

INFRASTRUCTURE

Senegal has a modern transportation network, including trains, buses, and international air service. There are 8,436 miles (13,576 km) of roads, out of which 5,968 miles (9,604 km) are unpaved. There are also 563 miles (906 km) of railways and 621 miles (1,000 km) of waterways, mainly on the Senegal River but also on the Saloum River.

Senegal has important ports at Kaolack, Ziguinchor, and Dakar. Dakar is the busiest port in West Africa and handles about 10 million tons (9,071,847 tonnes) of cargo every year. Its facilities include a tanker terminal, a container terminal, a grain shipping facility, a fishing port, and a dedicated phosphate terminal.

Dakar-Yoff International Airport is one of West Africa's major airports. There is also a local airport at Saint-Louis. After independence 11 West African countries joined together to form Air Afrique, which provides domestic flight service.

Senegal has 269,100 telephone lines, 4.123 million mobile telephone subscribers, and 820,000 Internet subscribers.

ENVIRONMENT

Mangroves found along the Sine-Saloum Delta

>S ENEGAL FACES MANY environmental challenges such as deforestation, soil erosion, depletion of fish stocks, coastal erosion, and open-air trash dumping. The key factor that has underpinned these challenges is a four-fold increase in Senegal's population in the short span of 50 years.

At the time of independence, in 1960, Senegal's population stood at 3 million. It is around 12 million today. Both the government and the people of Senegal have recognized the importance of developing a sustainable environment, but efforts to enhance environmental integrity have often been compromised by the growing needs of the exploding population, coupled with the people's need to earn a living.

FORESTS

Senegal has been losing its forests at an annual average rate of 111,197 acres (45,000 ha) since 1990. This adds up to 7.2 percent of its forest cover lost, or 7.9 percent if woodland habitats are included. The population explosion of Senegal has put pressure on the forests in two ways.

First there has been a tremendous rise in demand for traditional fuels, such as firewood and charcoal. Almost 63 percent of Senegal's energy requirements are supplied by such fuels, which are preferred by the rural villagers over gas or oil for basic needs such as cooking and lighting. This amounts to between on an average of 110,231 tons (100,000 tonnes) of wood cut down each year to serve as fuel.

Second there has been a rise in the demand for farmland. Acres of forests are burned down every year to make way for cash crop farming. In the 1960s the government proactively encouraged forests to be removed in order to make way for groundnut farms. Groundnuts have been Senegal's key export for years and groundnut farming was profitable to the point that the removal of forests became unregulated and extreme. Unfortunately groundnut farming has negative effects on soil. When harvested, the entire plant is taken out, roots and all, exposing the top soil to erosion. The other parts of the plant that are not needed—for example, the leaves and stems—are not plowed back into the soil to refertilize it, but instead are used as animal fodder. As a result the soil is easily exhausted and plantations frequently have to clear other forest areas and start up again, leaving waves of abandoned and dried-up fields in their wake.

Deforestation is made worse by Senegal's already unstable weather conditions. Senegal suffers from scarce and sporadic rains, having only one

Piles of firewood in a clearing. A greater demand for firewood has led to increasing deforestation.

A farmer prepares his land for cultivation. Environmental agencies have been trying to teach farmers more advanced ways to farm so that the land will not be exhausted.

rainy season that lasts between June and September. It also experiences frequent droughts. Deforestation and soil erosion, coupled with drought, have had clear visible impact on the forests in the Senegal River Valley, which have withered, and also on the expanses of oil palms in the Niayes and Thiès region, which have disappeared completely.

The government has acknowledged the problem of deforestation and has embarked on reforestation efforts. It aims to plant 5 million trees within a 74,132-acre (30,000-ha) area. In addition, it initiated the "Great Green Wall" of tree planting in 2005, which aims to plant a 4,375-mile (7,000-km) stretch of trees from Dakar through to Djibouti. Efforts have also been made to promote the use of gas instead of firewood and charcoal. In 2007, in a further effort to revitalize forests, the government shut down all mining operations in protected forest areas. Efforts will be made to find alternative sites for mining limestone, sandstone, and other minerals, so that the forests can be restored in peace. In addition, Senegal has one of the most comprehensive

Gazelles graze in the Guembeml Wildlife Reserve.

protected area systems in Africa, with 8 percent of its land protected. It has six national parks, six avifaunal reserves (places where the birds or the kinds of birds of a region, period, or environment stay all year round), and other protected forest reserves, including the Ferlo wildlife reserve, Reserve de Bandia, and Reserves de Popenguine.

OVERFISHING

Senegal's waters are being depleted of their fish stock due to overfishing. The annual sustainable catch in Senegal's waters is 462,971 tons (420,000 tonnes). But today about 496,040 tons (450,000 tonnes) of fish are removed from Senegal's water each year.

NATIONAL PARKS

Unlike other parts of Africa, Senegal is not known for its huge safari parks. It does, however, have a significant array of wildlife in its six national parks. Niokolo-Koba National Park, a UNESCO World Heritage Site, is the largest and serves as home to 80 species of mammals, 330 species of birds, 36 species of reptiles, 20 species of amphibians, and 60 species of fish. The park is a last refuge in Senegal for giraffes and elephants. It is also home to many "classic" African animals, including lions, chimpanzees, and antelope, some of which are rare, such as derby elands. The Parc National des Oiseaux du Djoudj, also a UNESCO World Heritage Site, is the third-largest bird sanctuary in the world. It contains a spectacular array of birds, as does Parc National de la Langue de Barbarie. The remaining three national parks are Parc National du Delta du Saloum, Il de la Madeleine, and Parc National de Basse. The latter is in Casamance and has been closed indefinitely due to rebel activity in the Casamance region.

The national parks are under strict protection, with surveillance posts to combat poaching.

The explosion in human population has been one factor in overfishing. Fish is a staple in the Senegalese diet and a four-fold jump in population has meant a rise in the demand for fish. Senegalese rely on fish for 75 percent of their protein needs. But the other critical factor that is perhaps more important is this: The fishing industry has become a key export earner for Senegal. Indeed the fishing industry has replaced the groundnut farming as Senegal's export leader in recent years. Income is earned by exporting the catch, as well as by selling fishing licenses to foreign boats that want to fish in Senegal's waters. These are typically boats from the European Union countries, because demand for fish that can be caught in Senegal's waters is high in those countries.

The combination of rise in local and foreign demand for fish has resulted in a significant decline in fish stocks. In 1989, 22,046 tons (20,000 tonnes) of conch were caught. By 1998 only 5,512 tons (5,000 tonnes) of conch were caught. Local fishermen are forced to go farther out to sea to find new fishing areas. Not only is this dangerous, as their small boats are not built to withstand deeper ocean waters, but it also results in slimmer profits as more time and fuel is spent traveling farther offshore.

Extensive environmental damage happens due to unsound fishing methods. As fishing stocks are depleted, desperate fishermen resort to techniques such as dynamite fishing and bottom trawling to reap their catch. In dynamite fishing, an explosive is thrown into a shoal of fish. The fishermen collect the dead fish that float up. Although this is expedient and quick, only one-quarter of the fish that are killed can be caught this way. The rest sink to the bottom. In bottom trawling, a large heavy net is dragged across the sea bed, stirring up huge billows of sediment. Other than catching fish, the net destroys vast numbers of corals and fish. In addition, foreign fishing boats are often unregulated. There have been reports that some fish without a license, others exceed their agreed-upon quotas, and still others target endangered species such as marine turtles.

In 2002 in an attempt to fix the situation, the Senegalese government banned foreign boats from fishing in its waters, refusing to renew fishing

An increase in demand for fish from Senegalese waters has led to overfishing.

Villages along the coast are under threat due to intense coastal erosion.

licenses. Although it later reinstated the licenses after much pressure and negotiation, it has pushed for greater regulation, though by and large, the enforcement of regulation has not been strict. The main dilemma is how to balance the profitability of the fishing industry with the environmental need to maintain the integrity and sustainability of Senegal's marine environment.

COAST

The coast of Senegal stretches 330 miles (531 km) and faces dramatic coastal erosion, leading to the destruction of property and homes. In Mbao, south of Dakar, a mosque fell into the water, while in Saly, tourist facilities had to be abandoned because of coastal erosion. In Rufisque, homes built along the coast have been sinking or are being carried away by the waters, forcing many people to abandon their homes.

The reason for coastal erosion is two-fold. First climate change has led to rising sea levels around the world. But the second and more critical reason is human activity. About 50 percent of Senegalese live along the coast because 90 percent of industry and services are located there. The population boom along the coast has led to the illegal extraction of sand from beaches to fuel the construction industry. For example, due to the real estate boom in Dakar, areas near Malika and Rufiesque have been hardest hit by illegal mining. Ironically the sand collected may not even be particularly suitable for buildings because its high salt content corrodes the metal skeletons of buildings. But illegal mining continues because it is lucrative, with some locals pointing out that they can earn more from carting sand from the beach to the construction sites than driving a taxi all day.

Human activity is also responsible for the chopping down of the coast's protective line of trees. This 168-mile (270-km) stretch of casuarinas trees from Dakar to Saint-Louis was planted by the colonial French between 1925 and 1949. Its purpose was to stem coastal erosion and prevent vegetable gardens from being sanded over. However, the booming coastal population has been using the wood of these trees as firewood for cooking or for making furniture.

Finally humans are responsible for the increasing amount of trash being dumped right on the beach front. As a result, places such as the U-shaped Plage de Hann, once one of the world's most stunning palm-lined beaches, is now Senegal's biggest environmental disaster, with factories regularly dumping their waste and sewage directly on the beach.

The government is trying its best to stem coastal erosion and pollution, but this requires a coordinated effort as this is a multifaceted problem. Better trash disposal techniques, better urban planning, the resettling of coastal communities, the enforcement of laws against illegal sand mining, and even the reforestation of the coastline are required. An environment squad has been set up with the gendarmes—soldiers who serve as an armed police force to maintain public order—to patrol the coast and watch out for illegal sand mining and garbage dumping. Coastal communities have also erected their own boulders, tires, and concrete walls to protect themselves and their gardens from the encroaching waves.

A pile of uncollected trash. Uncleared trash could have detrimental effects on the environment and well-being of the people.

TRASH

Senegal's cities produce 661,387 tons (600,000 tonnes) of waste per year. In Dakar alone, about 523,598 tons (475,000 tonnes) of household, industrial, and biomedical waste are dumped in an open-air dump site in Mbeubeuss, 15.5 miles (25 km) from the city center. The waste is not treated or sorted in any way. The Mbeubeuss dump site spans 1,482.6 acres (600 ha) and occupies a dried-up lake. The stench of the waste is very strong and the environmental effects are significant—the site could poison underground water supplies that provide nearby villages with drinking water as well as irrigation for local fruit and vegetable produce. Although villagers do complain, there are others who profit from the dump site. These are the scavengers who scour through the trash every day, picking up scrap metal, glass, plastic, and boxes to be recycled. Although they can earn up to three times the national minimum wage from doing this, they are also subjecting themselves to health risks, including tetanus, leprosy, scabies, and cholera. The government has announced plans for better dump sites that adhere to European standards of waste management. However, so far, none of these dump sites has gone beyond the early design stage.

SENEGALESE

A mother and her son in Saloum River Delta village.

IKE MOST AFRICAN COUNTRIES, Senegal is home to many different groups of people. Most Senegalese belong to one of seven major ethnic groups: the Wolof (43.3 percent), Fulani (Fulbe or Fulani) (23.8 percent), Serer (14.7 percent), Tukulor (9 percent), Diola (Jola) (3.7 percent), Malinke (Mandinka) (3 percent), and Soninke (1.1 percent). In addition to these, there are small numbers of French and Lebanese (1 percent).

In general, relations between these groups are peaceful, even cordial, with only occasional cultural conflicts. Most have lived

A group of friends. For the most part, the different ethnic groups of Senegal get along.

Despite the fact that the people of Senegal all come from different ethnic groups, relations between them are generally harmonious. Most Senegalese, like their other African counterparts, are Wolof, Tukulor, Fulani, Serer, Malinke, or from a minority group. In terms of clothing, it is the Wolof who have proven to be the most influential: most Senegalese have adopted aspects of Wolof dress.

Wolof women in Tambacounda wearing printed traditional dress and head wraps.

alongside one another for many centuries and rivalries have given way to mutual acceptance.

Relations between peoples are facilitated by a practice of mutual joking, which the Wolof call *kal* ("KAHL"). A Serer may tease a Tukulor by reminding him that the Serer were once slaves of the Tukulor. Other jokes might revolve around eating habits. Ethnic stereotypes become the subject of a friendly teasing that bridges the divide between people.

WOLOF

The Wolof make up 43.3 percent of the population of Senegal, or more than 5.5 million people. They are concentrated in the northwestern quarter of Senegal and The Gambia, their traditional homeland. It is believed that the

CHEIKH ANTA DIOP: A FAMOUS WOLOF

Cheikh Anta Diop was an Egyptologist and linguist who became one of the most influential African anthropologists. Diop was the founder of the Afrocentric movement, which traces the origin of humankind back to ancient Egypt. He developed a method of testing the level of melanin in Egyptian mummies, revealing that the ancient Egyptians were, indeed, black Africans. Painstakingly documenting the culture of the pharaohs as an authentic African culture with roots in the traditions of black Africa, Diop argued that early civilizations in the Nile Basin slowly fanned out across the continent, diversifying into the various African ethnic groups of today. This theory remains, at best, controversial among Egyptologists and American academics alike.

Wolof arrived in this region sometime during the 12th century, establishing the Jolof Empire, which quickly converted to Islam.

The Wolof are traditionally an agricultural people, but they have shown themselves to be adaptable in the face of change. Many have moved to the cities and adopted a modern lifestyle, working as civil servants, traders, or artisans.

The Wolof language, which is spoken by 80 percent of the population of Senegal, has been a major unifying force in the country. The Wolof have shown a great ability to influence those around them, to adapt to changing circumstances, and at the same time to maintain their distinctive culture. Because of these characteristics, they have taken an important role in forging a cultural identity for Senegal.

FULANI

The Fulani are a Pular-speaking group. They call themselves Fulbe but are known as Peul in French or Fulani in English. They are found throughout West Africa as far east as the Sudan, but their greatest concentration is in the northern part of Senegal along the middle reaches of the Senegal River Valley, where they live with the Tukulor, and in the northern Casamance.

Two Fulani women smile for the camera. The Fulani can be found throughout West Africa.

Their nomadic ancestors are thought to have come from a region north of the Senegal River. They have gradually migrated south and east over the last 400 to 500 years. During this time the majority of Fulani became sedentary, although there are also nomadic Fulani living in the Ferlo in small, isolated groups.

The traditional occupation of the Fulani is raising livestock. The Wolof, who appreciate the value of livestock but are more inclined to agricultural pursuits, frequently board their animals with the Fulani, who use the milk but give the manure back to the Wolof for use as fertilizer.

The sedentary Fulani are devout Muslims and tend to look down on their less devout nomadic relations. There is little ethnic cohesion among the different groups of Fulani, who have been separated by different lifestyles and diverse histories.

SERER

The origins of the Serer are unknown, but oral tradition shows that the Serer once lived with the Fulani and the Tukulor in the Senegal River Valley. In the 11th and 12th centuries, the Serer left that region when the others converted to Islam and settled farther south. When the Wolof established kingdoms in these southern areas in the 15th and 16th centuries, the Serer migrated to the Sine-Saloum and Thiès regions south and east of Cape Verde, the areas they occupy today.

The Serer are farmers. Their exceptional farming skills have made possible extremely dense settlements, the highest density in Senegal. In recent decades, however, population increases have put pressure on the productivity of the land, and many Serer have been forced to migrate in search of work, although few settle permanently in the cities. They are known as a hardworking and industrious people.

The Serer are among the most traditional people in Senegambia. They have been among the most resistant to Islam, often continuing today to follow traditional beliefs, and they have been slower than others to accept modernization. However, since independence they have undergone rapid Islamization and Wolofization. Serers migrating to Dakar are assimilating into the dominant Wolof culture, and many Serer in the peanut basin have adopted Wolof lifestyles after joining predominantly Wolof religious brotherhoods. The Serer's most famous son, Léopold Senghor, converted to Christianity.

TUKULOR

The Tukulor, like the Fulani, are a Pular-speaking group. They are concentrated in the Senegal River Valley. Their traditional land is the Fouta Toro, although they also live on the Mauritanian side of the Senegal River, as well as in Mali, Guinea, and other West African countries. Although the Tukulor were originally farmers, poverty has forced large numbers of them to relocate to other areas, particularly Dakar.

The Tukulor are thought to be the result of intermarriage between Serer and Fulani. They share a common language with the Fulani and social mixing

An African-Arab-Senegalese. Intermarriage between Africans and Arabs is a common occurence in Senegal today.

between the two groups is frequent. Their name is derived from the ancient kingdom of Tekrur. The Kingdom of Tekrur was founded by the Tukulor in the 11th century around the region of the Senegal River.

The Tukulor were among the first converts to Islam south of the Sahara in the 11th century. They take great pride in their religious fervor, and are critical of the influence exercised by predominantly Wolof religious brotherhoods on the country's political and religious life and the Wolofization of Tukulor living in Dakar. With the growth and development of irrigated agriculture, the Tukulor fear that their lands in the Senegal River Valley will be invaded by outsiders.

MALINKE

The Malinke, also known as Mandingo or Mandinka, are among the best known of West African peoples. There are large groups of Malinke in Senegal, Guinea, Ivory Coast, Mali, The Gambia, and Guinea-Bissau. Smaller populations are found in Liberia, Sierra Leone, Burkina Faso, and parts of Ghana. Altogether there are more than 5 million Malinke throughout West Africa. In Senegal the Malinke practice agriculture in the northern Casamance region, Tambacounda, and the southeast.

The name *Malinke* is a Fulani word meaning "the people of the ancient empire of Mali." In the 14th century Malinke culture spread from the edge of the Sahara south to the Atlantic coast and from the upper Senegal River to Hausa country in present-day Nigeria through the powerful Mali Empire.

A multiracial group of children congregates outside a Dakar school.

NON-AFRICANS

Although most of the French colonialists left Senegal after independence, a few chose to remain in the country. Others have come to Senegal to work for French firms on short-term contracts. During the colonial period, French people came as administrators, merchants, or technicians, remaining aloof from the native peoples and dominating the economic and political life of the region. Although today they are still a major force in trade and financial undertakings, the French no longer dominate politics.

In the 19th century the French encouraged Lebanese and Syrians to settle in Senegal to act as go-betweens for the French and their African subjects. Today the Lebanese and Syrians control a good part of Senegalese business, until recently dominating commercial, service, and production enterprises. They are involved in everything from large banking operations to small restaurants.

The *métis* ("may-tee") population, descended from marriages between European colonists and local women, were formerly an elite group who played an important role in Senegal's political, economic, and cultural life. The majority of métis have emigrated to France.

OTHER AFRICANS

Smaller African ethnic groups include the Bassari, Manjak, Lébou, and Diola. The Lébou, sometimes considered a subgroup of the Wolof, are farmers and fishermen in the Cape Verde region. Because they were the original inhabitants of Cape Verde, they own a lot of valuable land in Dakar and are generally more affluent than other Senegalese. They also dominate the fishing industry in Senegal. Due to their small numbers, the Lébou have become Wolofized, and some even consider themselves to be Wolof. The French granted the Lébou self-government during the colonial period, a right that they have retained to this day.

Compared to Lebou, the Bassari, at the other extreme, follow an isolated and traditional lifestyle in the Niokolo-Koba National Park, far removed from the influences of modern life. They continue to practice traditional religion and are known for their colorful initiation ceremonies.

The Soninke are a small group descended from the Berbers of North Africa. Increasingly they can be found migrating to towns, where they become small traders. Their ancestors founded the ancient Ghana Empire.

CLOTHING

The Wolof have set the trends in clothing style, as they have in many aspects of Senegalese life. Traditional dress for Wolof men, and in most cases for other Senegalese men, consists of baggy trousers and a *boubou* ("BOO-boo"), which is a loose, light, flowing robe with long sleeves. Many men wear a small cap.

At other times men might wear a *pagne* ("PA-nyuh")—a length of cloth wrapped around the hips—and a short-sleeved shirt.

Officials and well-to-do businessmen in the cities are more likely to wear European dress during the day and change to a boubou at home in the evening. Younger men are also more likely to dress in Western-style clothing.

Most Senegalese women wear a slightly different version of the men's boubou. Women's boubous are usually made of bright cotton and elaborately trimmed with embroidery or silk. They are complemented by brightly colored, showy hats or kerchiefs wrapped like a turban. Senegalese women wear jeweled amulets, necklaces, gold earrings, or other ornaments as accessories. For working around the house, women generally wear a blouse and *pagne*, or a loose cotton dress reaching almost to the floor.

Due to poor economic conditions in Senegal, some people can afford only a loincloth and shirt or simple dress. This style is much more common in rural areas where there is less wealth. However, beautiful clothes and elaborate ornaments are important to the Senegalese, and most people will make an effort to acquire the best clothing and ornaments they can afford and to wear their best outfits at every opportunity. Wolof women, in particular, are known for their love of fashion and ornamentation.

A village chief in Thiès dons a small cap and his wife wears a brightly colored boubou.

LIFESTYLE

A street scene in Dakar.

LIFESTYLE VARIES GREATLY IN Senegal depending on where people live and the group to which they belong. In the colonial period, urban residents enjoyed a completely different status from that of their rural brothers.

Africans born in the communes of Dakar, Gorée, Rufisque, and Saint-Louis were granted full French citizenship rights, while those who resided in other areas were considered "subjects." Subjects had few rights; they were subject to the *indigenat* ("AHN-dee-je-nah"), which enabled the military ruler to arrest and jail them without trial, to conscript them for forced labor crews, or to expropriate village land.

Many Senegalese living in the city iron clothes as a form of livelihood.

In recent times, many rural Senegalese have migrated to the cities in search of employment and a chance at bettering their lives and providing for their families. Rural communities in Senegal do not have ready access to health care and education. In the cities, however, life is not necessarily better. Many Senegalese are unable to find jobs and many live in shantytowns.

City dwellers, on the other hand, had access to education and employment in a wide variety of activities and participated fully in political life.

This division into two societies still influences Senegalese life. The life of a middle-class family in Dakar is worlds apart from that of a farmer in the Casamance.

VILLAGE LIFE

Rural living follows a traditional pattern that varies only slightly from one group to the next. Wolof villages, for instance, have 100 to 200 people grouped in compounds surrounding a village center, or *pencha* ("PAHN-cha"). A family compound, called a *ker* ("kair"), consists of a house or houses enclosed by a fence of dried palm fronds or millet or reed stalks. There is typically a house for the man of the household, situated at the entrance of the compound, and one for each of his wives. Small children and unmarried girls live with their mother; older boys live with their father. Houses are usually made of mud in a geometric shape (square or circular). There is a separate kitchen and both

A farmer tills his land.

A Senegalese woman hangs up laundry. Housing in shantytowns is often crudely constructed.

pit toilets and storage facilities are separated from the residential areas for reasons of hygiene. The women's work takes place in the shady courtyard in the center of the compound.

CITY LIFE

Dakar is characterized by extremes in housing. Upper-class neighborhoods, rivaling those of First World countries, are fully equipped with electricity, piped water, telephone service, and garbage pickup. Surrounding these are areas where houses have been crudely constructed and are overcrowded. In the suburbs, uncontrolled growth has led to the establishment of shantytowns or bidonville, where basic services may be entirely absent and housing is rudimentary—crude huts made of reeds or shelters improvised from packing crates, corrugated tin, or oil drums. These areas are populated mostly by recent migrants waiting to improve themselves. The shantytowns have become a major health problem. The combination of a lack of sewage and drainage

systems, no garbage pickup, and frequent flooding during the rainy season results in serious health risks for those condemned to live in these conditions. In 2008, 22 children in the Dakar suburb of Thiaroye/Mer died of lead poisoning. Further inspection by the World Health Organization revealed 71 more people with lethal levels of lead in their blood. The high levels of lead were due to the unregulated practice of lead recycling to make a living.

A man spinning cotton. Farmers who have moved to the cities are forced to take up a new trade.

MIGRATION

The majority of Senegalese continue to live in rural areas, although large migrations to the cities have been steadily changing the distribution of Senegal's population. In recent decades there has been a massive movement from country to city, mainly Dakar, in search of better living conditions, opportunity, and excitement. At the time of independence in 1960, 22 percent of the population lived in urban areas; in the mid-1990s more than 40 percent lived in the towns, with nearly 20 percent in Dakar alone.

Particularly during the dry season, large numbers of rural farmers make their way to Dakar in search of work. Some farmers return to their village and fields when the rains bring the return of agricultural work but others stay permanently, adding to the already overcrowded shantytowns on the edges of Dakar. This great influx of migrants has resulted in such rapid expansion that Dakar city services have failed to keep up with the increasing population.

SOCIAL HIERARCHIES

All the major ethnic groups (except the Diola) in Senegal traditionally followed a rigid system of social stratification determined at birth. Although the hierarchies are similar from group to group, there are a few main differences.

GRIOTS

Griots are a distinctive feature of West African life. Every important family kept a griot (gewel in Wolof) to serve as family historian and public relations officer. The griot advised the family on matters of lineage and acted as a court advisor and entertainer. His chief function was to sing the praises of his patron; in return the patron showered him with gifts. A griot prepared for his vocation by doing exercises to develop his memory and learning genealogies and histories of the great families, as well as learning to compose songs and play instruments.

Griots remain an important part of Senegalese life. The older ones are typically illiterate. They often have to travel constantly in search of sponsors who are able to pay for their services, since few families can afford the luxury of a personal griot. However, there are still a few griots who remain attached to one family, particularly among the Tukulor nobility. Some griots work as publicists for political parties or politicians, composing and singing songs praising their patrons or ridiculing rivals.

Tukulor society is the most complex, with 12 separate castes. The Serer, on the other hand, were an egalitarian society until the Malinke conquerors introduced them to their caste system.

Most Senegalese traditionally recognized three main strata: free people, artisans, and slaves. These strata were in turn divided into castes, which varied somewhat depending on the ethnic group. One's caste was the determining factor in the role one played in society.

With the social changes accompanying modernization, the caste system has lost some of its influence, but it is far from dead. Although slavery has been abolished, members of the slave castes are still despised. Most work as tenant farmers for their former masters, since they generally do not possess land of their own. Some may learn a trade and achieve some success, but their caste continues to dictate how others treat them. Marriage across castes is forbidden, and lying about one's caste is grounds for divorce. Political power continues to reside in the hands of the upper class. In more traditional areas, these distinctions may still be quite strong, while in Dakar they are less marked.

FAMILY RELATIONS

The extended family is the norm in most parts of Senegal. In rural areas, married sons and their wives have their own huts within the family compound. In cities, successful people are expected to play host to aspiring family members who approach them for aid.

Although Senegalese take their father's name, the matrilineage is almost more important, since land is passed on by the mother. Sons may work their father's land as long as they live with him, but eventually they must approach the patriarch of their mother's family to receive their own land. A special relationship exists with the mother's brother. In times of need, it is the mother's brother whom a Senegalese is most likely to approach for aid.

The matrilineage is dominated by the *tokor* ("tuh-CORE"), the oldest man. The *tokor* holds all the family money. Younger people who earn money give their earnings to the *tokor* to hold, and he administers the wealth of the family for the benefit of all. The *tokor* is also the person who must give permission for marriages. He receives the bride price that is traditionally paid to the bride's family.

A mother and daughter attend to daily chores together.

In order to keep the bride price in the family, often the daughter of a *tokor* is married to his sister's son.

Marriage may be arranged by the man's parents, or they may simply be asked to approve the couple's choice. In traditional arrangements, a go-between is asked to investigate the family background of the proposed bride. If it is a match, the go-between delivers kola nuts to the woman's parents. If they accept the marriage, they take the kola nuts. The imam— one who leads the prayer or a head of a community or group—performs the marriage in the mosque, while the bride and groom remain elsewhere.

It is even possible for marriages to happen without the knowledge of the husband-to-be. Some parents marry their son who is living abroad off, and then update him on his new marital status with a telephone call. After the religious ceremony, the bride is ceremoniously escorted to the groom's house by her relatives and friends, who drum, dance, and sing *mbalax*—pop music of West Africa with polyrhythmic percussion and dramatic vocal harmonies—tunes.

Women dance and sing at a traditional wedding ceremony.

Traditionally Senegalese are polygamous (men take several wives). The number of wives a man had was viewed as a sign of his wealth and status. Although Muslims are permitted to take up to four wives as long as they are able to provide for them, monogamy is becoming increasingly common, particularly among city residents. Men are now required by law (the Family Code of 1972) to declare at the time of the marriage whether the marriage is monogamous or polygamous. Still, as of 2005, half of all marriages in Senegal were polygamous, the highest rate in West Africa, with well-known Senegalese singer Youssou N'Dour marrying his second wife in 2006.

THE ROLE OF WOMEN

Senegalese women have made great strides since independence. With greater access to education and government policies instituted since the mid-1970s, Senegalese women now have the opportunity to take an active role in society.

During the colonial period, women were limited to traditional roles of food preparation and child care and had little access to education. In 1965 less than 1 percent of women could speak or write French. Today, although female literacy and school enrollment still lag far behind those of men, the gap is closing.

Senegalese women are taking a more active role in social and political issues today.

Women's progress in politics has been significant. They gained the right to vote in 1946, and the first woman deputy, Caroline Diop, was elected in 1963. Caroline Diop and Maimouna Kane became the first women to attain ministerial rank in 1978. Female representation in the National Assembly has risen from 12 percent in 1993 to 16 percent in 1998 and 19.2 percent since 2001. Now election rules stipulate that at least one woman must be elected rural councillor in every rural community. In 2002, 1,700 women were elected as local councillors.

Women's roles in urban areas are changing rapidly as they enter the labor market, generally as secretaries, typists, sales clerks, maids, and unskilled workers.

In rural areas, women are responsible for child care, meal preparation, and agricultural activities, although many are taking on greater responsibility outside their traditional roles. Increasingly they have become involved in managing village forestry resources, operating millet and rice mills, and helping to develop village health committees and prenatal and postnatal programs. Even those who mainly stay home may be involved in some form of commerce—for example, running a small street stall or selling jewelry.

Women's cooperatives are a significant way that women have used to gain autonomy. To join a cooperative, a woman pays a fee, the sum of which is regularly given to the member who needs it most—for example, to resolve financial difficulties or to support children's education. Cooperatives are also involved in advocating for women's issues, such as combating female circumcision or endorsing community work.

THE FAMILY CODE OF 1972

The position of women in the eyes of the law is defined by the Family Code of 1972. The Family Code forbids repudiation, the traditional Muslim practice that allows a man to formally divorce his wife simply by declaring them divorced. Women are allowed to own property, and in a no-fault divorce, restitution can be demanded. The code recognizes official as well as de facto marriages, and monogamous as well as polygamous marriages. When couples marry, they are required by the Family Code to sign a legal document stating the form of marriage they intend to establish— that is, either monogamy or polygamy. Once their choice is made, they cannot change their choice, even in the event of divorce—for example, if a couple who had opted for monogamy divorced, the man would not be able to enter a polygamous marriage after that.

The Family Code also establishes some important limits on women's rights by making the man the head of the household. Many women feel that the code fails to protect them sufficiently against forms of sexual harassment, especially domestic violence.

RITES OF PASSAGE

The Wolof, like other West Africans, observe two important rites of passage into mainstream Wolof society: the naming ceremony and initiation. The naming ceremony, called *ngente* ("gen-TAY"), takes place when a child is seven days old. At this ceremony, the newborn is officially given a name.

In rural areas, the day is celebrated by sacrificing a sheep, goat, or chicken. Family members and friends gather together and give gifts to both the child and mother.

Before the ceremony begins, the mother is washed. The infant's head is shaved and he or she is wrapped in white cloth. Later the call to prayer is whispered in the child's ear and the name is given. Afterward kola nuts are broken and shared, and pancakes and millet porridge are eaten.

As in most other African societies, a major event in every boy's life is his initiation into manhood. In most villages, all the boys of approximately the same age are circumcised together in a large group ceremony. Afterward they are isolated in one large room and are only allowed visits from adult males and elderly women.

During this seclusion period, they are taught sexual customs through special songs and sexual puzzles by the men who will act as their guardians. At the end of this instruction, a huge festival, called *samba sokho*, is held in the boys' honor.

YOUTH

Urban youth have become a source of concern to Senegal's leaders and community elders. Increasingly restless, alienated, and prone to violence, they were the main participants in and instigators of the 1988 post-election riots.

As unemployment figures rise among the young, frustration and violence are beginning to grow. Young people are the main force behind the public demand for *sopi* (the Wolof word for "change") in the Senegalese government.

But urban violence has not been their only response to a deteriorating society. In 1990 Dakar's youth initiated a spontaneous neighborhood cleanup campaign. Thousands of young people were mobilized to help clean up the slums and hovels of the capital. Hundreds of wall murals and other artwork now decorate buildings throughout the city, portraying health and environmental themes, important people in African history, and figures from Senegalese folklore.

HEALTH

Health and health care are major problems in Senegal. Except in a few cities, most Senegalese suffer from poor health, principally because of inadequate sanitation, poverty, and poor nutrition. In Dakar, four out of five people have clean water, but this proportion drops to one out of four in rural areas. Regular contact with polluted water and a lack of proper sewage systems put Senegalese at great health risks and these conditions spread chronic disease.

Schistosomiasis, a disease caused by a parasitic worm that enters the body through the foot when the victim goes in contaminated water, is extremely common, particularly in eastern Casamance and the central areas. Like malaria, schistosomiasis causes general debility and fatigue. Onchocerciasis, also called river blindness, is spread by tiny worms that migrate through the body and cause itching. In some cases, the victim is driven insane. Blindness results when the eyes are affected. In some areas, about 20 percent of the population is infected. Yaws, trachoma, and endemic syphilis are most common in the north and central areas. Malaria and yellow fever are also prevalent.

Health care is rudimentary outside the main cities. There are no clinics or hospitals in the rural areas. The statistics indicate that for every 100,000 people, there are six doctors, three pharmacists, and 0.8 dentists. Half of all health-care workers are concentrated in Dakar. Nevertheless the Senegal government has made an effort to improve health care by establishing mobile

A dispensary in Joal. Health care is not easily accessible to rural Senegalese.

hospitals and X-ray and laboratory facilities in an attempt to bring modern medical services to the rural areas. Life expectancy in Senegal is 57.08 years (55.7 years for men and 58.5 for women). The infant mortality rate is 58.9 deaths for every 1,000 live births, compared to the world average infant mortality rate of 49.4 deaths.

EDUCATION

In traditional Senegalese society, children learned the values and traditions of the community through the singing and dramatization of sacred myths. They began contributing to society at an early age, starting with simple tasks such as gathering wood or herding animals. At around eight years of age, they began to receive training in the occupation of their parents. Boys received a formal education at the local mosques, which consisted of recitation of the Koran, the Islamic holy book, and study of its teachings. Sometimes reading and writing in Arabic were included, but usually only for children of upper-class families. Girls generally did not attend school.

COLONIAL EDUCATION   The French introduced Western education to Senegal in the first half of the 19th century. Early schools provided instruction in French and manual skills. It was Louis Faidherbe who organized these scattered elementary schools into a state school system and added secondary education.

The education system was intended to train farmers, artisans, clerks, interpreters, and teachers to assist French administrators. When independence came, the Senegalese inherited a school system that closely followed the French system and produced a small number of highly qualified specialists. To some extent, this legacy has continued to hamper the Senegalese school system.

EDUCATION TODAY   Primary education is compulsory between the ages of seven and 13. However, family incomes often constrain children from attending primary schools. Primary school enrollment in 2003 was

59 percent, but actual attendance in school may be less since children may be enrolled, but may not attend school because they need to assist their parents in earning a living. In addition, because of a lack of government resources in education, pupils have to share books, notebooks, and pens. Sometimes schools do not even have a building. About one in seven children pass their exams at the end of primary school. Secondary education includes a first cycle of four years and a further cycle of three years. Secondary enrollment in 2003 was 24 percent for boys and 16 percent for girls, while tertiary enrolment was 4 percent. Ninety percent of students attend public schools. Koranic schools continue to supplement public education.

LITERACY Senegal still has a low rate of literacy and a marked difference between literacy rates for men and women. In 2002 the literacy rate was 51.1 percent for men and 29.2 percent for women. The fact that the native African languages are traditionally oral and have only recently been given a written form partially accounts for the low levels of literacy.

Elementary school students at class in Gorée.

RELIGION

Muslim Senegalese pray facing Mecca on a street in Dakar for Friday prayers.

N

NINETY-FOUR PERCENT OF ALL Senegalese are Muslim. About 5 percent of the rest are Christian, most of them Roman Catholic, and the remainder follow traditional African religions.

The conversion to Islam began in the 11th century, with the Tukulor being the first to convert. The new religion was introduced by the Almoravids, who came south from Morocco and Mauritania, spurred by the desire to spread their religion. Gradually Islam spread from one group to the next, through peaceful interaction or, more frequently, through armed conquest.

European colonization was, ironically, a great boost to the spread of Islam, as Islam became a center of resistance to European domination. On the other hand, Christianity spread slowly because of its association with the European colonizers.

Islam in Senegal has many distinctive characteristics. It has never entirely replaced traditional religions. Instead many people hold on to their African traditional practices, incorporating them into their Muslim beliefs.

ISLAM

Islam means "submission to God." The fundamental action of any Muslim is the public profession of faith, "There is no god, but God [Allah] and Muhammad is his prophet." It is this

Most Senegalese are Muslim and Islam's influence in the country is very apparent. Minority religions are able to practice without much opposition.

Right: A Muslim man prays with prayer beads.

The Great Mosque in Touba.

profession of faith that makes one a Muslim, and every Muslim repeats this statement of belief daily.

Islam is founded on what are known as the five pillars: recitation of the creed, daily prayers, fasting, giving alms, and making a pilgrimage to Mecca. All Muslims are required to pray five times a day at established times. These prayers may be private or communal prayers at the mosque. Every Muslim, except for people who are excused for health reasons, is expected to fast from sunrise to sunset during the month of Ramadan. This can be a demanding obligation when it falls during the summer, since Muslims refrain from drinking as well as eating during this time. Muslims are also obliged to give alms to the poor, and this is a compelling social obligation in Senegal.

Finally all Muslims are expected to make a pilgrimage (or hajj) to Mecca at least once, if they have the resources to accomplish this. The pilgrimage to Mecca is very important for Senegalese Muslims. Every year, 2,000 to 3,000 Senegalese make the hajj. Government officials arrange for transportation to minimize costs and paperwork. Some employers conduct lotteries so that one or more employees can win a trip to Mecca. Self-help associations are formed to pool resources and send one of their members to Mecca each year.

ISLAM IN SENEGAL

Islam has made steady progress in Senegal since the beginning of French colonial rule. In the colonial period, Islam served as the only viable alternative to complete French domination. For the Senegalese, Muslim leaders took the place of traditional structures of leadership that had been destroyed by the French and even led the resistance movement against the French.

Since independence, there has been an Islamic revival in Senegal, accompanied by a growing interest in Islamic theology, philosophy, and the Arabic language. Fundamentalism has been on the rise. This is partly encouraged by social and economic problems. But there has not been the kind of violent fundamentalism in Senegal that has surfaced in other countries in Africa and the Middle East.

The Senegal government has carefully controlled any tendency toward religious radicalism, outlawing political parties based on religious affiliation and supporting more reformist tendencies, while preserving its ties with the powerful brotherhoods.

Some tensions have surfaced between Muslims and Christians, although these have generally been minor clashes.

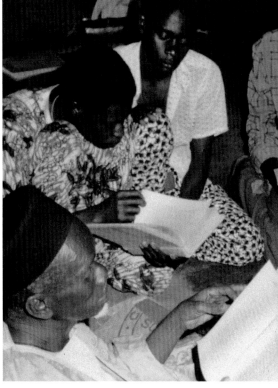

A group of Senegalese reading the Koran, Islam's holy book that contains the teachings of the Prophet Muhammed.

MARABOUTS AND BROTHERHOODS

Most Senegalese Muslims belong to an Islamic brotherhood. These brotherhoods arose as a result of Sufism, a mystical tendency in Islam that encouraged the rise of spiritual leaders, known as marabouts—holy men, called *serigné* ("seh-REE-nyay") in Wolof—who then gathered around them a group of followers. The followers saw their leaders as a path to greater communion with God. The brotherhoods that developed around these marabouts were hierarchically organized and based on the belief that marabouts could act as intermediaries between the ordinary Muslim and God.

Today marabouts often wield tremendous power. Part of the doctrine of the brotherhoods is based on the spiritual value of hard labor, and most brotherhoods require their members to contribute to the brotherhood. The

Supporters of marabout Serigne Bethio Thioune hold up his posters during a political meeting. Marabouts can hold a lot of political power.

head of the brotherhood holds all the profits accumulated by the brotherhood and is free to use this money as he sees fit. In addition, marabouts hold great political power.

There are three main brotherhoods in Senegal: the Qadiriyya, the Muridiyya, and the Tidjaniyya. They are distinguished by slight differences in ritual and codes of conduct. There is also a smaller sect called the Layene.

QADIRIYYA The Qadiriyya is the smallest brotherhood. It originated in Baghdad, with a principal influence in the Dakar-Thiès area and in parts of the Casamance. It is the oldest brotherhood in Senegal and was introduced by missionaries from Mauritania and the Niger River area to the northeast in the 18th and early 19th centuries.

MURIDIYYA The Mourides, as members of the Muridiyya are called, are the most tightly organized and influential brotherhood. Although not the largest brotherhood, they still number more than a million members. The Mourides were founded by Amadou Bamba M'Backe, a member of the Qadiriyya brotherhood, in the late 18th century. Bamba preached a gospel of work and established the Mouride practice of running peanut farms with the labor of *talibés* ("TAH-lee-bay"), the faithful. Bamba was succeeded by his oldest son, Falilou M'Backe, who ruled from 1945 until his death in 1968. He effectively consolidated hereditary rule within Mouridism.

The most influential of the *khalifas*—successors to the Prophet Muhammad's position as the political, military, and administrative leader of the Muslims—was Abdoul Lahat M'Backe, who ran the brotherhood from 1968 to his death in 1989. He was responsible for kickstarting the transformation of Touba, the Mouride center, from a small religious outpost into a major town of more than 500,000 people. He was a staunch supporter of Abdou Diouf during the 1980s. Today Touba is Senegal's second-largest city and a hub for global business, with Mouride businessmen importing goods such as refrigerators, televisions, and satellites for trade. It is also known as Little Mecca, attracting a million pilgrims annually. The current *khalifa* is Serigne Mouhamadou Lamine Bara M'Backe, who replaced his uncle, who died in December 2007.

TIDJANIYYA The largest brotherhood in Senegal is the Tidjaniyya. The Tidjaniyya were formed in 1781 by the Algerian Cheikh Ahmed Al Tidjani and reached Senegal around 1830. The brotherhood spread rapidly during the second half of the 19th century.

The Tidjaniyya follow one of three maraboutic houses. The oldest house goes back to Umar Tal, the Tukulor militant Islamic leader, that was built in Mali, Guinea, and Senegal from 1852 to 1864.

The most prominent house goes back to El Haj Malick Sy, a religious leader, and is based in Tivaouane. This house has a large following among the Wolof in the peanut basin, in the eastern regions originally settled by followers of Malick Sy, and in urban areas. The house has focused strongly on Islamic education, promoting the rapid spread of Koranic schools in the Thiès region. It has also established Koranic schools for girls.

Although the Mourides have the strongest following in the peanut-growing areas, they have also expanded in urban areas, and include many university students. The great majority of small traders in Dakar are Mourides, and Mouridism is also showing up in places such as New York, where Senegalese have migrated.

The third Tidjaniyya house was founded by Abdoullaye Niasse, a marabout blacksmith. This house, although less influential in Senegal, has millions of followers in Nigeria, Ghana, and elsewhere in West Africa. Unlike other brotherhoods, the Niasse house has not had good relations with the Senegal government. Ahmed Niasse founded Hizboulahi, the "Party of God," in 1979. It was immediately banned by the government as unconstitutional. Ahmed's brother started an Islamic newspaper that promotes an Islamic republic in Senegal.

CHRISTIANITY

Christianity, which was originally confined to the European settlements in Senegal, was fiercely resisted until the late 19th century because it was seen as the religion of the colonialists. The first mission was established in Dakar in 1845. Missionary efforts were most successful among the coastal Serer and the Diola in the southern Casamance. A primary attraction of Christianity for the Senegalese has always been the education offered by the church, which opened the door to modern careers, and thus became attractive even to Muslims.

Catholics have tended to gain positions of influence in Senegal, and thus the community has had more impact than its small numbers might suggest. Today 5 percent of the people say that they are Christians, and most are Roman Catholics.

TRADITIONAL RELIGIONS

There are still many believers in traditional religions, particularly among the Serer and the Diola, and small groups in the Casamance region. Among Muslims and Christians as well, many traditional beliefs have survived. Traditional African religions always include a supreme being who is all-powerful, timeless, and distant from humans. However, this being is rarely worshiped directly. Instead, natural objects and phenomena are used as agents of communion with higher spirits. These intermediary spirits may

The Niasses are the only brotherhood that has expressed any interest in forming an Islamic state. In general, it works with the existing government and limits its demands to greater Islamic content in the schools.

be benevolent or malevolent, but are believed to be swayed by prayer and sacrifice, and capable of punishing people through illness or madness.

Jinnehs ("JEE-nay"), or spirits, are thought to be either good or bad, and sometimes to dwell in cotton trees. They are also believed to haunt people, or influence them, sometimes causing madness, birth defects, and other deformities. The *Ninki-nanka* ("NEEN-kah-NAHN-kah"), a dragon-like snake, is thought to live in water and be covered with iridescent scales. The awe inspired by the Ninki-nanka is believed to kill a person on the spot.

Domas ("DOH-mah"), or witches, are men who are thought to attack and eat people, not through their own volition but rather because of a supernatural power inherited from their mother. Particularly dangerous times are childbirth for the mother and child, circumcision for the boy, marriage for the bride, and nightlife—social life during evenings—for the young man. Witches are also believed to seize souls during sleep or to enter the bodies of the sick. They are a source of great fear. People take many precautions against witches, and amulets worn to ward off witches are important for the Senegalese.

In addition to spirits present in the world, the souls of dead ancestors may intervene for the living. Sometimes they may be asked to intercede with the spirits to help their descendants. They are the guardians of tradition and morality and continue to be involved in daily events. Senegalese tend to believe in the existence of ghosts. These are generally people who have not been given a proper burial and are, therefore, restless.

AMULETS

Amulets are an important religious item for most Senegalese—both followers of traditional religion and Muslims. One of the major roles of the local marabout is to make and sell amulets. These consist of Koranic verses written on small pieces of paper and enclosed in a small leather bag that is worn around the neck or arm. They are believed to protect the wearer against witches, injuries, illness, and other misfortunes. The *jabarkat* fulfills a similar role, but is based in traditional practices. He also makes protective amulets, but these contain pieces of roots or plants.

A billboard in Dakar

A LTHOUGH THERE ARE 24 languages spoken within the borders of Senegal, linguistic diversity, like racial diversity, is not a serious problem for the country. Most of the languages are related, and there is much mutual intelligibility among them.

The main languages are French, Wolof, Serer, Pular, Diola, Mandinka, and Soninke. Eighty percent of the population speaks Wolof, 40 percent as their mother tongue and 40 percent in addition to their own native language. Generally people prefer to speak their native language at home and among friends, reserving French or Wolof for business and school. A small group—less than 2 percent—speaks Arabic.

Books published overseas are very popular in Senegal.

French is the official language of instruction in Senegal. However, besides the well educated, not many use or speak it, associating it with the colonial past and preferring to use Wolof alongside their own ethnic dialects. Due to the many languages of the country, newspapers, publications, and television and radio programs publish and broadcast in several languages.

A billboard for Sakan biscuits written in French.

African languages are historically oral and only recently have attempts been made to give them a fixed written form. In 1971 the government decreed the use of a modified Latin alphabet to transcribe the six major languages of the country. Dictionaries have been created for Wolof and Serer, a project that will be useful in standardizing spelling.

FRENCH

French is the official language of instruction, business, and government. Generally educated Senegalese speak French along with their native tongue, and some also speak English. A substantial part of Senegalese literature is written in French. It is still considered the unifying language of the country, although it is only the educated who speak French. Children generally are unfamiliar with the language, which puts great stress on the education system, which is entirely in French, and results in a high rate of illiteracy.

Most Wolof words can be seen in at least two different spellings, created by French and English transcribers. Pular is sometimes written in Arabic letters.

However, officials are reluctant to replace French as the language of instruction. This is because of the tensions that will likely arise if the government is forced to adopt the language of one of Senegal's many ethnic groups as the official language. They also fear that replacing French would isolate Senegal from the rest of the world, since the unifying language would then most probably be one that is almost entirely limited to Senegal.

WOLOF

Wolof is, on a practical level, the unifying language of the country. Some 80 percent of the population speaks Wolof, although the language has no official status. It is the primary language of 40 percent of the population (the Wolof and Lébou), the rest speaking it as a second language. Dakar and other urban areas have become relay centers for dissemination of the language. At Ziguinchor in the Casamance, for instance, more people know Wolof than any other language, although the majority of the population is not Wolof.

A newspaper carrying headlines written in French. French is the official language of instruction in the country.

Although most Senegalese speak Wolof, few people outside of Senegal speak the language, and most of these are people of Senegalese origin residing in France. The Dakar Wolof dialect, which is rapidly becoming Senegal's unofficial national language, absorbs or Africanizes many French words and European concepts into its vocabulary. Wolof is part of the West Atlantic subgroup of the Niger-Congo family of languages, which includes all of the major African languages spoken in Senegal.

MANDINKA

Mandinka is part of the Mande subgroup of the Niger-Congo family of languages. It is easy to learn and was an important unifying factor in the creation of the Mali Empire. Today it is still widely spoken in West Africa. It is estimated that there are about 5.3 million people in West Africa who speak Mandinka as a first or second language. Mandinka is a tonal language, with high, medium, and low pitches being used to give different meanings to words that sound alike. Sarakole and Bambara are the other important languages of the Mande subgroup spoken in Senegal.

PULAR, SERER, AND DIOLA

Pular, also known as Fulbe, Fula, Fulani, or Peul, is also part of the West Atlantic subgroup of the Niger-Congo family, although it was once considered to belong to a different Niger-Congo group. Pular speakers are found over an immense area, as far east as Chad. Estimates set the number of speakers

Fulani women. The Fulani people speak Pular, one of the most widely spoken languages in Senegal.

at 11.5 million, and the language is spreading. The Tukulor speak a dialect of Pular. Pular is the principal language of the Senegal River Valley.

It is surprising that Pular is spreading so rapidly, because it is an extremely complex language. Pular is characterized by "alternation," where both the beginnings and endings of words go through changes according to grammatical function. By contrast, in Latin, which is considered to be a complex language, only the endings of the words are changed.

Other languages of the West Atlantic subgroup of the Niger-Congo family spoken widely in Senegal include Serer and Diola. Serer is spoken in the Thiès and Sine-Saloum regions. Diola is the primary language of the Casamance. The two most important Diola dialects are Fogny and Kasa. Fogny is used by Radio Dakar and understood by most Diola. Fogny is spoken in the area around Ziguinchor.

THE MEDIA

A newsboy holds out a copy of *Sud Hebdo*, a weekly paper devoted to politics, business, and current affairs.

Senegal was the first of the French West African territories to have a press. *Le Moniteur du Sénégal* (*Senegal Monitor*) was founded in 1854 and was followed by the *Journal Officiel de la République du Sénégal* (*Official Journal of the Republic of Senegal*). Today *Le Soleil* (*The Sun*), a French language daily newspaper, is available in all the main towns in the morning. It is sponsored by the government. *Sud Hebdo* (*South Weekly*) is a weekly newspaper that focuses on politics, current affairs, and business. *Walfadjiri* is a Wolof weekly devoted to current affairs since 1994. *Le Devoir* (*Obligation*) is a bimonthly, also on current affairs. *Le Cafard Libéré* (*Boredom Liberated*) is a satirical weekly paper. All in all, there are 20 daily newspapers, including privately owned *Sud Quotidien* (*The Daily South*) and *Le Quotidien* (*The Daily*).

Senegal's radio and television stations used to be run by Office de Radio-Telediffusion du Senegal (ORTS), the national government-controlled radio and television network, but since 2003 control of the media was liberalized and there are now four private TV stations along with several private radio stations. In July 1994 SUD FM became the first private radio station to go on the air. Compared to the rest of West Africa, Senegal enjoys one of the most unrestricted press climates in the region, with the media frequently criticizing the government.

A Senegalese man listens intently to the radio for news on the presidential elections in 2006.

GREETINGS AND GESTURES

In urban areas, Senegalese most commonly greet one another by shaking hands or kissing three times on alternate cheeks, a custom similar to French tradition. In rural areas, people shake hands, but traditionally, men do not shake hands with women.

When taking leave of others, Senegalese again shake hands or kiss cheeks, as well as extend best wishes to family members and mutual friends. It is customary in Senegal to engage in small talk about work, health, family, and mutual friends before coming to the point of any meeting.

In traditional families, children and women curtsy to older people to show respect. Senegalese avoid eye contact with a person they consider superior either in age or status. It is impolite to ask personal questions. In addition, Senegalese avoid asking specifics regarding children (how many one has or their ages). This is considered bad luck.

THE IMPORTANCE OF GREETINGS

Senegalese place great importance on greetings. Each time you meet someone during the day, it is important to spend some time—maybe a good 10 minutes—greeting him or her in order to show respect. To pass directly to the business at hand or to pass by with a simple wave of the hand, even if the other person is engaged in another activity, would be considered unbearably rude. Significantly, a Senegalese who is angry with someone is likely to express his anger by refusing to greet the other person. This shows lack of respect or outright contempt for the other person and is treated as a great insult. When one Senegalese was asked why he repeated the other person's family name over and over in greetings, he explained that he was acknowledging the other person's entire family, including ancestors as well as the living.

A typical greeting conversation might go as follows:

As-salaam alaikum!—a traditional Muslim greeting meaning "Peace!"

Peace is with you!

Did you spend the night in peace?

In peace, thanks to God.

How are you?

Oh, my friend, I'm here.

How are the people of the house?

They are there.

How's your father?

He's there.

How's your mother?

She's there.

Do you have peace?

Peace only, thanks to God.

Inquiries about the health of the family and friends may go on for a considerable length of time, a practice that has given rise to jokes about greetings in which inquiries are made regarding the state of health of the family goat. The length of these greetings indicates the great importance placed on human relationships, particularly family, in Senegal.

ARTS

A craftsman starts to carve a wooden statue.

Senegal has a
rich art tradition.
Traditional
crafts are still
practiced, and
the contemporary
arts scene
continues to
develop
and flourish.

>S ENEGAL HAS AN ASTONISHINGLY rich artistic tradition. For a small, impoverished country, it has made an amazing contribution to the world of art. In addition to traditional arts, Senegalese artists have also achieved international recognition in literature, filmmaking, and popular music.

Traditionally Senegalese have viewed art in functional terms rather than for its intrinsic value. For instance, storytelling, although it may serve as entertainment, is primarily a vehicle for communicating social values and history and for educating children in the ways of the group. The Wolof word for "beauty" may be translated as "that which is suitable;" thus the work of art is judged on its appropriateness for a particular end rather than for its aesthetic value. Works of art are valued not for their individual beauty, but for the meaning that is invested in them. Representational likeness is not highly valued; instead meaning may be indicated by abstract markings that are understandable by only a few. The communal function of a performance is generally more important than the quality of individual performance.

Right: A woman engraves a gourd under a tree.

TRADITIONAL CRAFTS

The Wolof people are well known for their skilled craftsmanship. Crafts were traditionally assigned to specific castes that specialized in these areas, such as smiths, weavers, dyers, leather workers, woodworkers, basket weavers, and potters. These craft-worker castes were generally accorded low status in the social hierarchy, although their work was often highly regarded. Most traditional crafts are objects needed for everyday use, such as pottery and baskets.

Particular specialties in pottery are the large water jar, or *ndal* ("dal"), and the *anda* ("AN-dah"), a perforated incense burner. Wolof pottery is made of red clay with patterns in charcoal black or chalk white. A pyramidal cover closes the mouth of pots. Pottery figures are valued as decorative items.

Woodcarving is another specialty of the Wolof. Mahogany is sculpted into various forms to express the wishes of the artist. The sculpture is polished black or brown. Sometimes pieces are decorated with ivory, cattle tails and horns, feathers, and other natural objects.

Colorful baskets, mats, and lamps made from palm fronds for sale.

In addition, the Wolof create striking geometric and organic designs on cloth, either handwoven or machine made. Other woven crafts include baskets and fences made from palm fronds. The Bambara are known for their extremely fine mats with woven geometric patterns. The Bambara also produce cloth designs by dying fabric with a background color and then bleaching out intricate patterns.

The Fulani are known for their leather work, which is often dyed in bright colors, punched, carved, or embroidered. Most designs are geometric, in keeping with Islamic prohibitions on representational art. Generally Islamic restrictions on representational art reinforced a preexisting tendency toward abstraction in Senegalese art.

Masks on display. The art of mask making is slowly disappearing.

Jewelry created by Serer and Malinke craft workers is of such high quality that it has found its way into museums in Senegal and France. Originally created for Wolof women, who place great value on personal adornment, these gold and silver bracelets, necklaces, earrings, and pendants in delicate filigree have shown little change through the last several hundred years.

The art of mask making, formerly an important facet of Senegalese life, has declined with the disappearance of old rituals. Many artisans today are abandoning their crafts, although the government has made efforts to support the production of traditional crafts.

MUSIC

Music is an important part of Senegalese life, being used for both social and religious functions. Much of the daily work in the villages and rural areas is

Traditional instruments are used even in modern music today.

accompanied by music and singing. In other situations, music tends to be associated with group dancing rather than independent performances.

The chief traditional music uses percussion instruments, particularly drums. The art of drumming is highly respected and very popular. This music uses a wide variety of drums to produce tonal contrasts. The *tamal* ("TAH-mah"), a drum shaped like an hourglass, is held under the arm. Varying the pressure of the arm produces different tones. Xylophones, rattles, gongs, and bells are other common percussion instruments. The *balafon* ("bah-lah-FONE") is a wooden gourd-resonated xylophone.

Traditional stringed instruments include the *kora* ("KOH-rah"), a 21-stringed harplike instrument used in southern Casamance, and the *xalam* ("HAH-lam"), a type of lute. The *xalam* consists of a resonator (usually made of a gourd) over which cowhide is stretched. Most have five strings, except the *molo* ("MOH-loh"), which has only one string. Wind instruments include whistles, horns, and flutes.

European music has been disseminated in Senegal through the schools and Catholic missions, and has had some influence on native music. Popular

YOUSSOU N'DOUR

Youssou N'Dour was born in Dakar in 1959 and began singing as a child performer at neighborhood gatherings in Dakar. He made his professional debut at the age of 12, and was soon singing regularly with the Star Band, then the most successful group in Senegal. In 1979 he formed the Étoile de Dakar, which was succeeded in 1981 by the Super Étoile, now the most famous band in Senegal. In 1986 Super Étoile toured with Paul Simon, and the following year, it accompanied Peter Gabriel on his world tour. Super Étoile also played at the Amnesty International World Tour in 1988.

N'Dour made his international debut in 1994 with the single "7 Seconds," a duet with Neneh Cheery that became a smash hit and won a Grammy nomination. He is the best-known Senegalese music star in the world, winning the Contemporary World Music Grammy Award for his album Egypt in 2005 and the Critics' Award at the World Music Awards the same year.

Although he is an international star, N'Dour continues to draw inspiration from his Senegalese roots. He is a pioneer of mbalax, an up-tempo blend of African, Caribbean, and pop rhythms. Most recently, in 2007, he made his film debut in the movie Amazing Grace, a story about William Wilberforce and the abolition of slavery in 18th-century Britain.

Baaba Maal, like Youssou N'Dour, has achieved an international reputation as a popular singer. Born in northern Senegal to Tukulor parents, Maal has taken upon himself the calling of the griot, even though he was not born into that caste. His music is called yela *("YAY-lah"): a traditional form that mimics the sound women made when pounding grain. Women performing the* yela *would hit the stressed third beat on their calabashes, while others clapped on the weaker first beat.* Yela *dates back to the empire of Ghana, when Senegalese kings used it to call the people of the empire together.*

Maal has produced nine albums, the best known being Lam Toro *and* Firin' in Fouta. *He sees himself as a spokesperson for his people: "In Senegal people will not excuse me if I sing a song and it does not say anything; because I've had the opportunity to study and travel and they haven't. I'm an African, I belong to a universal civilization, and I grew up in music even though I'm not a griot. I know I have a responsibility to help society to make choices."*

Senegalese music has been heavily influenced by American, French, and Cuban music, although since the 1970s it has tended to move more in the African direction. Popular artists such as Youssou N'Dour, Baaba Maal, and Touré Kunda have achieved enormous success both in Senegal and abroad, and have created a new, unique, Senegalese style of popular music. Often these modern groups incorporate traditional Senegalese instruments and pay homage to the griot tradition, sometimes including griots in their band.

Griots often played in groups of three or four drums, flutes, and rattles. Modern Senegalese music has its roots in the griot ensembles.

LITERATURE

In precolonial West Africa, the primary means of education and record-keeping was through oral literature, including trickster tales, dilemma tales, proverbs, riddles, and puzzles. The griots acted as the guardians of this oral tradition. Some examples of the griot tradition have been preserved in Birago Diop's *Contes d'Amadou Koumba* (*Tales of Amadou Koumba*, 1947). In this important work of Senegalese literature, which won the Grand Prix Littéraire de l'Afrique Noire in 1964, Diop recounts tales told to him as a child by his family griot, Amadou Koumba. Diop is particularly known for his skillful rendering of dialogue and gesture.

Diop was one of the most important of the first generation of modern Senegalese writers, along with his compatriot, Léopold Sédar Senghor. Senghor was the chief originator (along with Aimé Césaire from Martinique and Léon Damas from French Guiana) of Negritude, a literary movement of the 1930s, 1940s, and 1950s against the French colonial policy of assimilation. Through Negritude, Senghor asserted the value and dignity of African traditions and peoples. Senghor is known for his lyric poetry, especially the collection *Chants d'Ombre* (*Shadow Songs*, 1961).

Other important Senegalese writers include Ousmane Soce, David Diop, Alioune Diop, Cheikh Amidou Kane, Abdoulaye Sadji, Abdoulaye Ly, Ousmane Sembene, and Bakary Traore. Soce's *Karim*, which tells the story of a boy growing up in early 20th-century Senegal, is one of the most widely read pieces of modern African writing. Contemporary writers such as Boubacar Boris Diop are more critical of contemporary life. Important women writers include Mariama Ba and Aminata Sow Fall.

Writer Léopold Sédar Senghor (*left*) with then-mayor of Paris, Jacques Chiraq (*right*).

PAINTING

Originally heavily influenced by European art, in the 1960s Senegalese painting began to develop its own style called École de Dakar, or Dakar school.

Aminata Sow Fall is best known for her novel La Grève des Battus *(The Beggars' Strike, 1979), which recounts the disastrous results after government official attempts to rid Dakar of its beggars.* L'Appel des Arènes *(The Call of the Arenas, 1982) is the story of a boy whose parents raise him outside his family and community. In 1997 Mount Holyoke College in the United States granted Aminata Sow Fall an honorary degree in recognition of her literary work.*

Well-known painters of this school include Dioutta Seck, Maodo Niang, and Amadou Ba.

Native painters have developed a uniquely Senegalese specialty: reverse glass painting. Called *sower* ("SOW-air"), the paintings are made by self-taught painters who draw images onto the back of a transparent glass surface, lending the image radiance and protection. In a humorous style, glass painters depict the daily life of ordinary Senegalese, which can be seen in shop windows, buses, or on any available piece of glass. The best-known sower artists are Moussa Sakho, Babacar Lo, and Gora Mbengue.

FILM

Senegal is the capital of African Cinema, with Senegalese filmmakers producing an astonishing range of excellent films in spite of a lack of production facilities in Senegal and a very limited audience. Some established filmmakers include Ousmane Sembene, Djibril Diop Mambety, Moussa Sene Absa, Safi Faye, Khady Sylla, and Joseph Gai Ramaka. Notable films worth highlighting include *Karmen Gei* (2001), a film by Joseph Gai Ramaka that tells the classic story of Carmen in the Senegalese context—this is Africa's first filmed musical, replacing Bizet's music with indigenous Senegalese music and choreography; *Hyenas* (1992) by Djibril Diop Mambety, a parable based on the classic play *The Visit* by Frederich Durrenmatt; and *Moolade* (2007) by Ousmane Sembene, a film addressing the topic of female circumcision.

OUSMANE SEMBENE

Born January 1, 1923, in Ziguinchor, Ousmane Sembene rose from a poor and obscure beginning to become perhaps the greatest Senegalese artist of all time. Through his novels, and even more through his films, he introduced Senegal to the world.

Sembene spent his youth as a fisherman on the Casamance coast. In Dakar, he worked as a bricklayer, plumber, and mechanic before serving in the French army in 1939. He joined the Free French Forces and eventually ended up in France, where he remained, working as a docker in Marseilles and teaching himself to read and write French. His first novel, Le Docker Noir (The Black Docker), was published in 1956. A spinal disorder forced him to make writing his livelihood, and he soon completed O Pays, Mon Beau Peuple! (O Country, My Beautiful People!), Les Bouts de Bois de Dieu (The Twigs of God, recounting a railroad strike and the fight to combat colonialism), Voltaïque, L'Harmattan, and Xala.

Around 1960, frustrated with writing only for the literate elite, Sembene turned to filmmaking in an attempt to reach the Senegalese masses. In 1966 he made his first feature film, The Black Girl, which was also the first feature-length film to be produced by an African filmmaker. It won a prize at the 1967 Cannes Film Festival. Sembene's last film was Moolade in 2004, which focused on the controversial topic of female circumcision. Moolade won prizes at the Cannes Film Festival and the Venice Film Festival. Sembene died at age 84 in June 2007, and is widely referred to as the Father of African Cinema.

LEISURE

Wrestling is one of Senegal's favorite events and is not only a sport but also has ceremonial significance.

LEISURE IN SENEGAL VARIES WIDELY between town and country. Urban centers afford entertainment similar to that found in any large Western city. In the country, Senegalese engage in more traditional leisure activities. Nevertheless a few leisure activities are popular throughout the country. Generally Senegalese like to sit and talk in their leisure time. Telling or listening to stories is a traditional leisure activity that is still popular.

RELAXING IN CITY AND COUNTRY

The Senegalese are especially fond of movies, their country being a great producer of outstanding films. Where there is electricity, concerts, discos, and videos provide additional pastimes. Dakar offers a wide range of entertainment. Live, open-air concerts take place regularly. Clubs provide young people with a place to enjoy contemporary African music.

In rural areas, work and leisure are structured by the seasons. The period after the harvest provides a long rest for farmers. They take advantage of this time to visit relatives, often traveling to Dakar to avail themselves of the hospitality of migrant relatives. Dancing and family and village celebrations are often used to fill this time.

Leisure activities differ in rural and urban areas. In rural areas where electricity is not readily available, Senegalese may spend more time visiting their family and friends. In the city, many Senegalese enjoy watching movies, attending concerts, and going to popular nightspots. Generally all Senegalese enjoy sports—soccer and wrestling in particular.

Children playing soccer on the beach.

SPORTS

The most popular sport in Senegal, as in most of Africa, is soccer. Often played as a street game, soccer is a popular pastime, particularly among children. Soccer was introduced by the French around World War I and has since spread from the urban areas throughout the country. Each village has its own youth team, and the country has a soccer major league where teams representing different regions compete for the national championship.

Senegal burst onto the African soccer scene when it beat Nigeria in the semifinals of the African Cup of Nations in 1992. In 2002 Senegal scored a huge upset by defeating the world and European champion, France, 1—0 in the Fédération Internationale de Football Association (FIFA), World Cup's opening game. The national football team, Lion of Terangas, made it to the quarter finals that year, becoming only the second African nation to do so (the first being Cameroon in 1990). The team's star player, El Hadji Diouf, was named one of 2002 World Cup's Top Ten Players and was put on the World Cup All Stars Team.

Unfortunately, since 1992, Senegalese soccer has been on the decline—a professional league was promised, but never materialized, with rumors arising that the Federation Senegalese de Football was mismanaging funds. In January 2008 the Lion of Terangas was knocked out at the state level of the African Cup of Nations, prompting most of the Federation's officials to resign. FIFA and the Senegalese government have since stepped into organize elections, restore the Federation's credibility, and create a professional league.

Other popular sports include basketball, cricket, and track and field. Jogging has become a very popular activity in the cities as a way to keep fit. In the morning and evening, young and old alike can be seen jogging and doing exercises. The Corniche Ouest in Dakar has a running track that attracts large numbers of Senegalese, usually in the hours before and after work.

STORYTELLING

An important traditional activity in Senegal, and throughout West Africa, is storytelling. The storyteller was important not only for his or her power to amuse, but also as the keeper of tradition and history.

Christian Ododo of Nigeria (*left*) and Souleymane Camara of Senegal (*right*) struggling for the ball during the African Cup of Nations in 2006.

WRESTLING

The traditional Senegalese sport is wrestling, or laamb *("lambe," in Wolof). Sometimes described as a combination of wrestling and judo, it is typical of traditional African wrestling. There are two types of* laamb: *one in which wrestlers are allowed to hit one another with their hands, and a more acrobatic type that does not allow hitting.*

But laamb *is not only a sport; it is also valued for its ceremonial aspects. Each wrestler is accompanied by his marabout. In a ceremony that precedes the match, the wrestler wears various kinds of amulets on his arms, legs, and waist, and dances around the arena to the music of drummers and singers. All of this ritual is intended to protect the wrestler against evil spirits and any witchcraft that might be used by other wrestlers.*

Wrestlers usually come from lower-caste backgrounds and serve as champions of their ethnic group or region. Each wrestler tries to intimidate his opponent by boasting of his skill and past victories. Each brings with him an entourage of drummers and praise singers who build him up and denigrate his opponent.

Long ago, wrestling matches were held at night or in the afternoon in the main square of the village. Accompanying the wrestling match was much singing, dancing, and storytelling. Today laamb *takes place mostly on Saturday or Sunday evenings, but it remains Senegal's national event.*

The best-known type of traditional West African story is the animal trickster tale, in which animals are used to represent certain qualities. Leuk the Hare represents cunning and wit; Bouki the Hyena is the thief; Choi the Parrot is the gossip; and Gayndeh the Lion represents courage. Leuk the Hare crossed the Atlantic with West African slaves and entered American literature as Brer Rabbit. In addition, *kouss* (leprechauns), *konderong* (dwarves with long beards), and *doma* (witches) are frequent characters in West African tales. These tales were used to transmit the values and traditions of the society, as well as to while away the time during the slow period after the harvest.

Participants gather for a street dance.

DANCING

Dance is an important leisure activity in Senegal and the principal means of self-expression for the Senegalese. Elaborate ritual dances were formerly performed on special occasions, such as celebrations marking life-cycle or seasonal changes or the start of a hunting expedition. In these instances, dance formed an important part of a larger religious ceremony.

Today dance is considered an important part of the traditional heritage by educated urbanites, while it continues to form part of daily life in the villages. The Senegalese dance readily: at religious ceremonies, social or political gatherings, or just for the pleasure of it.

Dance is generally expressive, interpreting a mood through body movement rather than prescribed footwork or gestures, although there are some precise traditional forms. Dances are most commonly performed by groups of dancers moving in lines to instrumental music and chants. The national dance company, which is associated with the national theater, is particularly well respected and has toured internationally.

FESTIVALS

Men playing *koras* during a festival in Dakar.

>S ENEGAL CELEBRATES CHRISTIAN, Islamic, and traditional African festivals. However, organized public festivals are rare. Feast days, marriages, and naming ceremonies are important celebrations to the Senegalese, but they are generally celebrated in private.

ISLAMIC HOLIDAYS

Islamic holidays follow the Muslim calendar, which shifts back by 11 days every year in relation to the Gregorian calendar. Just as with other important Muslim practices, festivals are the same for Muslims all over the world. There are, however, a few practices that are unique to Senegalese Muslims.

The most important part of the year for Muslims is the month of Ramadan. For the entire month, all adult Muslims who are in good health are required to fast from dawn to dusk. Muslims rise before dawn to eat an early meal. Then, after it becomes light, they refrain from eating and drinking until darkness falls again. After dark, they eat a big meal and celebrate until late

Right: A military parade through Saint-Louis on Independence Day.

115

PUBLIC HOLIDAYS

January 1	New Year's Day
March/April (variable)	Good Friday
March/April (variable)	Easter Monday
April 4	National Day
May 1	Labor Day
May (variable)	Ascension Day
May (variable)	Whit Monday
July 14	Day of Association
August 15	Assumption
November 1	All Saints' Day
December 25	Christmas
(variable)	Korité
(variable)	Tabaski
(variable)	Mawloud

into the night. Ramadan is a time for extra attention to prayers, study of the Koran, and spiritual reflection.

At the end of Ramadan comes Id al-Fitr, or Korite, as it is called in Senegal. Korite begins with the first sighting of the new moon and can last for two days. Muslims dress up in brand-new clothes and spend the day making visits to family and friends. This is the most important holiday of the Muslim year.

Id al-Adha, or Tabaski, as it is known in Senegal, is the second official Muslim holiday. It marks the time of the hajj, the pilgrimage to Mecca that all Muslims are urged to undertake sometime during their life. For Tabaski, the head of the household sacrifices a lamb to celebrate Abraham's willingness to sacrifice his son as stated in the Bible. Parts of the lamb are distributed to the poor. The head and feet are smoked and preserved for the New Year's celebration about a month later. The dinner for Tabaski is usually *mechoui*, whole roast sheep.

There are also two lesser Muslim holidays: Mawloud and the Islamic New Year, called Tamkharit in Senegal. Mawloud marks the anniversary of the Prophet Muhammad's birth. Many people make a pilgrimage on this day to the tomb of an important marabout. The most important of these is the pilgrimage to Tivaouane, the capital of the Tidjani brotherhood. At Tamkharit, Allah (God) is believed to determine each person's destiny. Muslims prepare for the holiday with a short fast and ablutions to purify themselves, obligatory components of the Islamic prayer ritual. Rites on that day emphasize prosperity in the New Year. It is believed that sharing food with the poor will help bring a good year. A festive meal featuring couscous, coarsely ground semolina pasta, with a smothering of vegetables, mutton, and gravy is often eaten for the New Year.

Musicians play calabashes as guests dance in celebration of the New Year.

Pilgrimages are an important part of Muslim life in Senegal. The most important of these is Magal, the annual pilgrimage of the Mourides. Magal celebrates the symbolic return of Cheikh Amadou Bamba, the founder of the Mourides, to the holy city of Touba, which he founded. Bamba was exiled by the French and spent his last years in Djourbel, unable to return to Touba.

Magal, like other Muslim holidays, follows the lunar calendar. Every year hundreds of thousands of pilgrims come to Touba, arriving by car, bus, train, and on foot. The focus of the festival is a night of prayer either in the main mosque or with individual marabouts. Other brotherhoods also have annual pilgrimages, much the same but smaller than Magal.

TRADITIONAL CEREMONIES

A battle with masked attackers is part of the Bassari initiation ceremony.

Many people in Senegal still practice some type of traditional initiation ceremony. In the Thiès region, girls who have come of age perform a *syniaka* ("see-nee-AH-kah") dance to celebrate the end of a week-long seclusion. This takes place in May, and at one time included circumcision, although this is no longer practiced. In the Casamance, the Bassari initiation ceremony (called Nity) includes a fire dance in which the initiate's old personality is ritually burned. The festival features elaborate costumes and a ritual battle with masked attackers for boys undergoing initiation. This is preceded in March by Olugu, a jubilant entry of initiates from the previous year, signifying their reintegration as adults. The Diola celebrate their initiation of boys, called Futampaf, in May and June.

Many people celebrate the harvest with a festival. In the Casamance, sheaves of rice are offered to the gods at the festival of Beweng and permission is asked to store the freshly picked crop. Dancers wear feathered costumes,

The Fanals festival takes place in Saint-Louis during the Christmas season, from December 21 to January 1. It dates from colonial times, when the principal religion of Saint-Louis was Catholicism. Christmas Eve Mass was an important social event, and wealthy women of mixed race, called métis ("may-tee"), would compete to see who had the richest gowns and jewelry. Because the gowns were quite long and heavy, the women brought pages to support their trains and also to carry lanterns to light their way. During the service, the pages would hold their own competition outside the church to determine who had the most artfully constructed lantern.

Today there are no more ladies in rich gowns, but the lantern competition has survived. Sponsored by local businessmen, the lanterns are built by clubs. Then the elaborate lanterns, made of split bamboo, paper and cardboard, silver foil, gilt, tinsel, and colored cloth, are paraded through the streets of Saint-Louis. The designs are spectacular, in shapes of ships, airplanes, buildings, monuments, masks, and even replicas of mosques or a patron's house.

beaded and tassel-decked arm and leg bands, flamboyant headdresses, and flowing garments.

The festival of Ekonkon in the Casamance celebrates fertility and productivity, as men and women leap around like acrobats in a display of agility. In O Lumata, also in the Casamance, ritual dances help acolytes communicate with the dead and the gods. Trance-inducing drugs and rhythms are used to help the communication along.

In Thiès in June, the Kunyalen festival is celebrated with exhortations to the gods and colorful dances. Rituals are performed to ensure female fertility and to protect newborns. At Fil in June and July, songs, poems, and stories are used to predict good crops and a healthy future for the village. At Ebunaay, women are the main performers. There are dances for a week, which culminate in the selection of a beauty queen.

The Casamance celebrates the feast of the king of Oussoye, called Zulane, in May. In July, Zumebel is celebrated with a wrestling match between young girls.

FOOD

A woman selling produce at a stall in Dakar.

CHAPTER 13

SENEGALESE FOOD IS SIMPLE, for the most part. Most days the average Senegalese will eat rice with fish. In rural areas, where food is scarce, meals may be extremely simple—just a millet mash with a spicy sauce over it for flavor. This food is prepared by the women, who spend long hours searching for leaves to flavor the sauce, pounding the millet in large mortars in the open courtyards of family compounds, and then slowly cooking the mash over an open fire.

Although years of French domination have left a certain French influence, particularly in the urban areas, North African and Middle Eastern cuisines have had a greater effect. Lebanese immigrants have opened many small restaurants and snack bars in Senegal, which have popularized Middle Eastern cooking. North African specialties such as couscous have also been adopted. French bread and café au lait are always popular.

MEAL PATTERNS

Breakfast is eaten between 6:00 and 9:00 A.M., lunch from noon to 1:30 P.M., and the evening meal between 8:00 and 9:30 P.M. Typical breakfast

Although most Senegalese dishes are simple, they draw influence from the differing ethnic groups that reside within Senegal's borders, as well as from the French and other immigrants. The abundance of fish has made fish a staple in the Senegalese diet. Rice also features in many Senegalese dishes. The people of Senegal eat with their hands, instead of with utensils.

121

foods include *rui* (pap—a traditional porridge made from mielie-meal, (ground corn or other grain), *churra* (porridge), or fried foods such as *akara* (fried beancake), *yokhos* (fried oyster), or *jen* (fish). Residents of Dakar are likely to have bread, a pancake with coffee or sweet tea, or leftovers from the previous meal. Lunch or dinner typically consists of steamed rice, millet, or couscous with a stew of vegetables, nuts, or meat. Millet is the most common grain in the rural areas and among the less affluent. The upper class generally eats white rice, giving this a prestige value. Rice consumption in the country has doubled in the last 20 years.

The most typical middle-class urban meal is rice and fish. Since rice, unlike millet, requires no pounding, it is also popular among women, who are typically responsible for food preparation. Millet, sorghum, and corn are all pounded in large wooden bowls, then boiled to make a mash and seasoned with various spices. The variety in this diet, the basics of which remain the same from one day to the next, is to be found in the sauces used.

Workers at a street restaurant preparing dishes for their customers.

Farmers join together to beat millet in the fields.

Affluent people in the urban areas have access to many European items, which add variety to a basic Senegalese diet. The French influence is noticeable in the Senegalese taste for French bread, dressed salads, and appetizers. For dessert, Senegalese prefer a slice of fresh fruit, perhaps pineapple or papaya. Mango is also a popular desert.

INGREDIENTS

Fresh fish is common in Senegal, including barracuda, tuna, sea bass, mullet, Nile perch, swordfish, devil fish, and sole. Seafood is also prevalent, including prawns, crabs, lobsters, crayfish, sea urchins, and oysters. Lamb is the most common meat; beef is eaten sometimes. Christians and animists also eat pork, but milk and meat of any kind are eaten rarely in Senegal due to economic constraints, except in large cities and among the Fulani, who are traditionally herders. Popular vegetables and herbs cultivated in the coastal areas are cabbages, carrots, spring onions, leeks, turnips, pumpkins, eggplants, spinach, garlic, parsley, mint, and cilantro. Sorrel, dried baobab leaf, and okra are also used. Tropical fruit, such as mangoes, watermelons, melons, guavas, passion fruit, grapefruit, limes, bananas, and soursop—a fruit with green skin, black prickles, and white flesh—are plentiful.

SENEGALESE DISHES

One favorite Senegalese dish is a Wolof invention called *cheb-ou-jen* ("CHEB-oo-jenn"), or rice with fish. *Cheb-ou-jen* is made with several varieties of fresh fish, sea snails, dried fish, and vegetables seasoned with chili peppers. "*Cheb* joints," where workers can pick up *cheb* (short for *cheb-ou-jen*) on their lunch break, are a common sight in urban areas. These are small, makeshift kitchens with a huge iron caldron sitting on a brush or woodburning container of fire. Here housewives cook for their families, selling the remainder to passersby.

Preparing *cheb* is a complicated procedure. First, deep slits are cut into thick fish steaks, which are then stuffed with a spice mixture called *roff*. The

Women select their fish at the fish market.

fish is browned lightly, after which the vegetables are cooked in a large caldron. After the vegetables are cooked, rice is cooked in the same caldron. A brown crust of rice forms on the bottom of the pot. This crust, considered a delicacy, is served with the *cheb*.

Stuffed fish, called *poisson farci* ("PWAH-so fahr-see"), is often part of *cheb*, but it can also be served on its own. It is a specialty of Saint-Louis. This usually uses mullet, which is filleted and flayed, leaving the skin removed in one piece. The flesh is chopped finely and spiced, after which it is sewn up in the skin, and the whole package is baked.

Millet is the basis of dishes such as *ngalakh* ("GAH-lak," millet, peanut paste, and baobab fruit, sweetened with orange-flower water), *chakri* ("CHAH-kree," steamed millet balls eaten with sweetened yogurt), and *lakh* ("lahk," millet porridge).

Chicken *yassa* (a chicken stew) is a specialty of the Casamance. Traditionally made with chicken, it can also be made with any type of meat. The meat is marinated in lemon juice, pepper, and onions.

Riz Jollof ("ree joh-LOHF," Jollof rice) is common in Senegal, as well as all over West Africa. It consists of a mound of vegetables and meat in a tomato sauce on rice.

Chicken *yassa* is a dish from the Casamance.

In rural areas, meals often consist of rice or millet mash with a sauce. Sauces such as *mafé* ("MAH-fay") or *domodah* ("doh-moh-DAH") are based on tomatoes and peanuts. The most common sauces use wild leaves for flavoring.

SNACKS

Small roadside or market stalls called *dibiteries* ("DEE-bee-tree") serve lamb, beef, or liver kebabs with bread and a pepper sauce. These are really butcher shops, where you choose your cut of meat, which is then chopped and barbecued on the spot. Another popular snack is *chawarma* ("sha-WAHR-mah"), which is made of shreds of barbecued, compressed mutton cut from a roll and wrapped in pita bread. These are found in *chawarma* bars. There is also *merguez* ("mehr-GEHZ," a spicy sausage), *kofta* ("KOF-tah," meatballs), *fataya* ("fah-TIE-yah," ground meat and onion pies), or *nems* (a pancake roll made of vermicelli).

A small fish shack along the beach.

Senegalese enjoy drinking mint tea.

DRINKS

Drinks include *bissap* ("BEE-sahp"), which is made from hibiscus flowers, ginger drink, *ditakh* ("DEE-tah," a green fruit infusion), lemongrass tea, and *kinkeliba* ("kin-keh-LEE-bah," a medicinal drink). *Bouille* ("BOO-yah") is sherbety baobab juice and tamarind juice is also popular. *Niamban* ("nee-AM-bahn") is a mixture of tamarind juice, smoked fish, salt, and cayenne. In the Casamance, palm wine is the traditional drink. The French café au lait is popular for breakfast.

The Senegalese end their meals with mint tea, made from green tea and fresh mint. This tea is brewed three times and guests are expected to stay for all three servings. The first is strong and bitter, the second sweeter, and the third sweeter and milder. The drinking of mint tea is an important social function in Senegal. In leisure moments, Senegalese often spend their time conversing over pots of mint tea.

CUSTOMS

Hospitality is an important custom in Senegal, and meals served to guests are specially prepared well in advance.

The Senegalese serve food on a large, flat tray. A mound of rice is placed on the tray, and then vegetables and fish are arranged over the top. The whole tray is then placed on a mat on the floor. Family members sit around the tray, serving themselves from the central dish.

A bowl of water is prepared ahead of time and used before and after the meal for washing the hands. People use their right hand to eat, rolling a little rice with fish and vegetables with the first three fingers, squeezing this into a ball, and popping it into the mouth.

A father teaches his children how to eat with their hands.

A schoolgirl washing her hands.

The hostess usually breaks off pieces of meat or vegetables for her guests. Occasionally some urban Senegalese follow French customs, eating at tables and using plates and silverware, but this is not the norm.

Children are taught early to clean their hands thoroughly, and to eat only from the part of the communal dish that is directly in front of them. They are also told to avoid eye contact with anyone while they are still eating, as it is considered impolite.

The left hand is only used when necessary but never to put food into the mouth, because it is considered unclean in Islamic culture. For instance, one might hold fruit in the left hand while peeling it with the right.

In traditional homes, people eat in separate groups according to age and gender. Diners pour water over their hands as they enter the dining area and then wipe them on a common cloth.

CHEB-OU-JEN (RICE WITH FISH)

Roff (paste):

2 bunches of flat-leaf parsley

1 sweet pepper, seeded and minced

4 scallions

1 bouillon cube

4 cloves garlic

1 tablespoon oil

Purée ingredients together until smooth.

Fish:

3—4 pounds (1½—2 kg) whole fish

2—3 inches (5—7 cm) oil, for deep-frying

Use a sharp knife to cut deep slits into the fish, but do not slice all the way through. Stuff the slits with the roff. Heat the oil in a large, heavy pan or pot, and brown the fish on both sides. Remove the fish and drain on absorbent paper.

Sauce:

3 onions, finely chopped

2 cans tomato paste

3 bouillon cubes

6 cups (1½ liters) water

1 package tamarind paste

Drain the pot of all but a few tablespoons of oil. Add onions, bouillon cubes, tamarind paste, tomato paste, and water. Let this simmer.

Stew and Rice:

1 calabash

2 hot peppers

5 small sweet potatoes

2 green peppers

8 okra

1 pound (½ kg) dried cod

3—4 chili peppers

1 cup (250 milliliters) rice per person

Chop vegetables, except okra, into large chunks. Add vegetables and cod to the sauce and cook for 30 minutes or until tender. Add stuffed fish for the last few minutes of cooking. Remove vegetables and fish with a slotted spoon and place in a container. Cover to keep warm.

Measure the liquid remaining in the pot. Add or remove water for the amount of rice to be cooked (you need 2 cups [500 ml] of water per cup [250 ml] of white rice). Add rice, bring to a boil, then cover and simmer until done.

To serve, spread rice on a large platter and distribute fish and vegetables over it evenly. Reserve some sauce to pour over the rice and vegetables. Garnish with lime wedges.

MAMADOU'S BANANA GLACE

Serves 8

12 bananas

1 pint (625 ml) heavy cream

½ cup (125 ml) sugar

½ tsp (2.5 ml) chopped candied fruit

1 tsp (5 ml) black raisins

1 tbsp (15 ml) chopped peanuts

1 tbsp (15 ml) slivered almonds

8 red cherries

Using an electric blender, blend four bananas, the heavy cream, and sugar until frothy. Pour the mixture into a tray and freeze for one to two hours until partially firm. Then slice the remaining eight bananas in half lengthwise and then in half across. Place each sliced banana (four pieces in a row side by side) on an individual-sized dessert plate. Spread the frozen banana mixture uniformly over the fresh bananas when ready to serve. Sprinkle each serving with the candied fruit, peanuts, and almond, and top each serving with a red cherry.

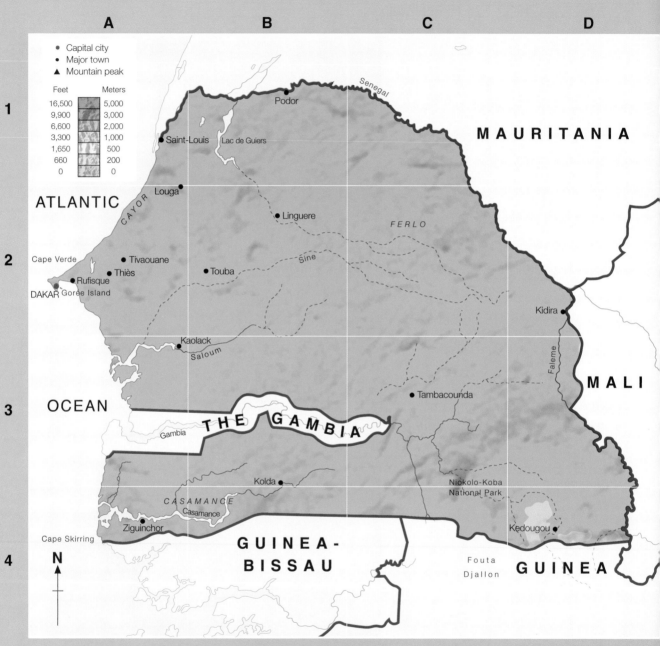

A   B   C   D

- Capital city
- Major town
- ▲ Mountain peak

Feet	Meters
16,500	5,000
9,900	3,000
6,600	2,000
3,300	1,000
1,650	500
660	200
0	0

1

2

3

4

MAURITANIA

Senegal

Podor

Saint-Louis

Lac de Guiers

ATLANTIC

CAYOR

Louga

Linguere

FERLO

Cape Verde

Tivaouane

Thiès

Touba

Sine

Rufisque

DAKAR   Gorée Island

Kidira

Kaolack

Saloum

Falémé

MALI

OCEAN

Tambacounda

THE GAMBIA

Gambia

Kolda

Niokolo-Koba
National Park

CASAMANCE

Casamance

Ziguinchor

Kedougou

Cape Skirring

GUINEA-
BISSAU

Fouta
Djallon

GUINEA

N

MAP OF SENEGAL

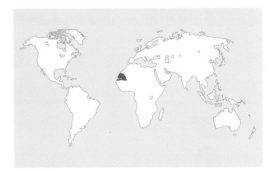

ECONOMIC SENEGAL

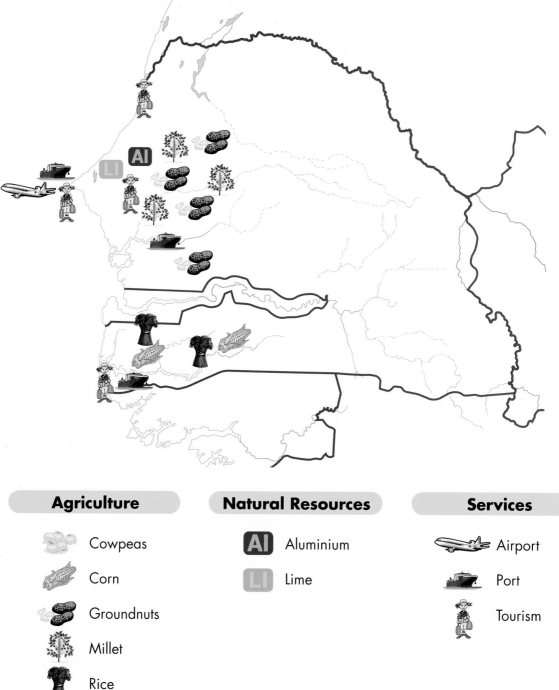

Agriculture	Natural Resources	Services
Cowpeas	Al Aluminium	Airport
Corn	Li Lime	Port
Groundnuts		Tourism
Millet		
Rice		

ABOUT THE ECONOMY

OVERVIEW

Senegal is considered a good economic performer by the World Bank, with the fourth-largest economy in West Africa, after Nigeria, Ghana, and Côte d'Ivoire. It has achieved an annual growth rate of about 5 percent since its currency devaluation in 1994 and poverty has declined from 68 percent in 1994 to 51 percent in 2005. However, Senegal remains a poor country with unemployment hovering around 48 percent for the past few years. The average worker earns only $840 a month and Senegal continues to rely heavily on foreign assistance, which comprises 23 percent of annual government spending, or $630 million, from countries and organizations like France, the United States, European Union, China, the IMF, World Bank, and the African Development Bank.

GDP (PURCHASING POWER PARITY)
$21.02 billion

GDP (OFFICIAL EXCHANGE RATE)
$11.12 billion

GDP GROWTH
4.6 percent

CURRENCY
USD 1 = 518.218 Communaute Financiere Africaine Franc (XOF) (2009)

LAND USE
Arable: 12.51 percent, Permanent Crops: 0.24 percent, Others: 87.25 percent

AGRICULTURAL PRODUCTS
Groundnuts, millet, corn, sorghum, rice, cotton, tomatoes, green vegetables, cattle, poultry, pigs, fish

MAJOR EXPORTS
Fish, groundnuts, petroleum products, phosphates, cotton

MAJOR IMPORTS
Food and beverages, capital goods, fuel

MAIN TRADE PARTNERS
France, Mali, Netherlands, China, UK, Italy, India, Thailand, The Gambia, Belgium

WORKFORCE
4.85 million

UNEMPLOYMENT RATE
48 percent

INFLATION RATE
5.9 percent

EXTERNAL DEBT
$2.19 billion

CULTURAL SENEGAL

Parc National de la Langue de Barbarie
This national park is frequently visited by tourists and birdwatching enthusiasts due to its close proximity to Saint-Louis and its abundance of bird life.

Parc National des Oiseaux du Djoudj
The Parc National des Oiseaux du Djoudj, also a UNESCO World Heritage Site, is the third-largest bird sanctuary in the world. It contains a spectacular array of birds, as does Parc National de la Langue de Barbarie.

Gorée Island
Gorée Island, just east of Dakar, was declared a historical site in 1951. Its ancient buildings played a significant role in the slave trade.

Grande Mosque
Built in 1964, the Grande Mosque in Dakar is impressive for its sheer size and landmark minaret.

Palais Presidentiel
The Palace in Dakar was built in 1907 for the governor at the time, General Roume. It has beautiful gardens and guards in colonial-style uniforms.

Touba
Touba is a holy city that attracts millions of pilgrims from the Mouride Brotherhood annually. Its mosque is one of the most impressive places of prayer in the whole of West Africa.

Niokolo-Koba National Park
Niokolo-Koba National Park is a UNESCO World Heritage Site. It is the largest and serves as home to 84 species of mammals, 350 species of birds, 36 species of reptiles, 20 species of amphibians and 60 species of fish. The park is a last refuge in Senegal for giraffes and elephants. It is also home to many "classic" African animals, including lions, chimpanzees, and antelope, some of which are rare, e.g., derby elands.

ABOUT THE CULTURE

OFFICIAL NAME
Republic of Senegal

FLAG DESCRIPTION
The flag is made up of three vertical bands of equal width, in green, gold, and red. In the center band, there is a star with five branches.

TOTAL AREA
75,749.4 square miles (196,190 square km)

CAPITAL
Dakar

ETHNIC GROUPS
Wolof (43.3 percent), Pular (23.8 percent), Serer (14.7 percent), Jola (3.7 percent), Mandinka (3 percent), Soninke (1.1 percent)

RELIGIOUS GROUPS
Muslim (94 percent), Christian (5 percent, mostly Roman Catholic), indigenous beliefs (1 percent)

BIRTHRATE
36.52 births per 1,000 population

DEATH RATE
10.72 deaths per 1,000 population

AGE STRUCTURE
0—14 years: 41.9 percent (male 2,717,257/ female 2,668,602)
15—64 years: 55.1 percent (male 3,524,683/ female 3,552,643)
65 years and over: 3 percent (male 183,188/ female 206,886) (2008 est.)

MAIN LANGUAGES
French (official), Wolof, Pulaar, Jola, and Mandinka

LITERACY RATE
Total population: 39.3 percent
Male: 51.1 percent
Female: 29.2 percent

LEADERS IN POLITICS
Léopold Senghor (1960—80); Abdou Diouf (1980—2000), Abdoulaye Wade (2000—)

POPULATION
12,853,259 (2008 est.)

TIME LINE

IN SENEGAL	IN THE WORLD
	323 B.C. Alexander the Great's empire stretches from Greece to India.
	1206–1368 Genghis Khan unifies the Mongols and starts conquest of the world. At its height, the Mongol Empire under Kublai Khan stretches from China to Persia and parts of Europe and Russia.
1617 France established its first permanent settlement in Senegal, on Goree Island.	
1756–63 Seven Years' War	
1848 French government abolished slavery.	**1789–99** The French Revolution
1891 Senegal proclaimed a French colony.	
1895 Senegal becomes part of French West Africa.	
1902 Capital of Senegal moved to Dakar.	
1914 Blaise Diagne elected as Senegal's first African deputy to French parliament.	**1914** World War I begins.
	1939 World War II begins.
1945 Senegalese women granted the right to vote.	**1945** The United States drops atomic bombs on Hiroshima and Nagasaki.
1946 Senegal becomes part of the French Union.	
1956 National Assembly established.	
1957 Africanization of the administration.	
1960 Senegal becomes independent.	
1963 First constitution drawn up.	

IN SENEGAL	IN THE WORLD
1966 Senegalese Progressive Union becomes country's sole political party.	
1970 Abdou Diouf appointed prime minister.	
1976 Constitution amended. Three-party political system introduced.	
1981 Abdou Diouf becomes president. Mouvement des Forces Démocratiques de Casamance (Democratic Forces Movement of Casamance) formed.	**1986** Nuclear power disaster at Chernobyl in Ukraine
1989 Dispute over grazing rights in southern Mauritania sparks violent unrest in Senegal and Mauritania.	
1997 Government signs peace accord with separatist rebels in Casamance, but fighting continues.	**1997** Hong Kong is returned to China.
2000 Opposition leader Abdoulaye Wade wins second round of presidential elections.	
2001 Government signs peace accord with separatist rebels in Casamance. Léopold Senghor, founding father of Senegal, dies at age 95.	
2002 President Wade fires the prime minister and the rest of the government.	**2003** War in Iraq begins.
2004 Fighting with rebel separatists continues despite peace accord.	
2006 The army launches an offensive against rebels from a faction of the Casamance Movement of Democratic Forces.	
2007 President Wade wins reelection.	

GLOSSARY

balafon ("bah-lah-FONE")
A wooden gourd-resonated xylophone.

boubou
A loose, light, flowing robe with long sleeves.

cheb-ou-jen ("CHEB-oo-jenn")
A Wolof dish of rice and fish.

domas ("DOH-mah")
Witches; men thought to attack and eat people because of a supernatural power inherited from their mothers.

griot
Member of a caste of historians who keep the records of families in the form of oral history.

hajj
A pilgrimage to Mecca that all Muslims are supposed to make once in their lives.

harmattan
A dry, dusty wind that blows in from the Sahara.

jihad
Islamic holy war fought by Muslim leaders against the French colonizing forces.

ker ("kair")
Fenced compound with a house or houses.

laamb ("lambe")
Traditional Senegalese wrestling; a cross between wrestling and judo.

marabouts
Leaders of religious brotherhoods, generally thought to have a great deal of social and political power.

métis ("may-tee")
Afro-Europeans descended from marriages between European colonists and local women.

pagne ("PA-nyuh")
A length of cloth wrapped around the hips and worn by men and women.

pencha ("PAHN-cha")
Village center.

sower ("SOW-air")
Paintings depicting daily life in Senegal.

syniaka ("see-nee-AH-kah")
A dance performed by girls after their coming of age ceremony.

tamal ("TAH-mah")
A drum shaped like an hourglass.

tokor ("tuh-CORE")
The oldest man in the family; the family head.

xalam ("HAH-lam")
A type of lute.

yela ("YAY-lah")
A traditional form of music that mimics the sound women make when they pound millet.

FOR FURTHER INFORMATION

BOOKS

Ross, Eric S. *Cultures and Customs of Senegal*. Westport, CT: Greenwood Publishing Group, 2008.

Gritzner, Janet H., and Gritzner, Charles F (ed.). *Senegal*. Philadelphia, PA: Chelsea House Publishers, 2005.

WEBSITES

BBC News, Country Profile: Senegal. http://news.bbc.co.uk/1/hi/world/africa/country_profiles/1064496.stm

CIA The World Factbook: Senegal. http://www.cia.gov/library/publications/the-world-factbook/geos/sg.html

Senegal Tourist Office New York. http://www.senegal-tourism.com/

FILMS

Hyenas. Djibril Diop Mambety, 1992.

Karmen-Gei. Joseph Gaï Ramaka, 2005.

Moolaadé. Ousmane Sembene (Director), 2004.

Youssou N'Dour: I Bring What I Love. Elizabeth Chai Vasarhelyi, 2008.

MUSIC

Egypt. Youssou N'Dour, Nonesuch Records, 2004.

Rokku Mi Rokka. Youssou N'Dour, Nonesuch Records, 2007.

BIBLIOGRAPHY

Dio, Birago. *Tales of Amadou Koumba*. London: Oxford University Press, 1996.

Koslow, Philip. *Senegambia: Land of the Lion*. Philadelphia: Chelsea House, 1997.

Sallah, Tijan M. *Wolof* (Heritage Library of African Peoples). New York: Rosen Publishing Group, 1996.

Sembene, Ousmane. *God's Bits of Wood*. London: Heinemann, 1996.

Sweeney, Philip. *The Gambia and Senegal*. Singapore: Insight Guides, 1996.

INDEX

INDEX